ARMS
BEYOND
DOUBT

ARMS
BEYOND
DOUBT

THE
TYRANNY
OF
WEAPONS
TECHNOLOGY

Ralph E. Lapp

Cowles Book Company, Inc.
New York

Contents

Military-industrial complex / Involvement of science / Eisenhower's views on the complex / The defense triangle / Politics of the complex / The U. S. war machine / Fallibility of the Pentagon / Defense domination of Congress / The new militarism / The funding process / L. Mendel Rivers / Incompetence of staff members / Congressman Moorhead's defense dinosaur / Sen. Cooper's Elizabethan scholar / The Senate and technology / The instrument of fear / Research open-endedness / Technological forecasts / Control of military spending / Post-Vietnam budgets.

The aerospace complex / California defense contracts / Top ten contractors / Project Camelot / Lack of scientists in Congress / The weapons scientists / Technological innovation / Wall Street and science stocks / Lockheed, General Dynamics, and L-T-V / Corporate plans for defense business / U. S. aerospace sales / Galbraith on defense business / Defense socialism / Retired officers in defense companies / Civilian officials shuttle to Pentagon / The C-5A contract award / Cancellation of major weapons systems / Pentagon mistakes / MOL / Future weapons systems / AMSA / Impact of defense industry.

Momentum of A-bomb development / U. S. atomic proposals / Buildup of U. S. nuclear stockpile / The thrust of technology in weaponry / Need for arms controls / Nuclear scorpions / Nuclear proliferation / Arms treaties / SALT talks / Arms limitations / Inspection problems / U. S. techno-militarism / Arms cutbacks and fear of first strike / Need for self-control / National priorities / Influence of Red China / The control of fear.

ARMS BEYOND DOUBT

I

Of Arms and Men

Cavemen, slinking around in the gloom of man's prehistory, displayed more sense about weapons than modern man. Maybe they had a favorite cudgel or two, but they did not stockpile overkill.

Today, weapons have become our major industry and we torment ourselves with doubts about the sufficiency of immense stockpiles of nuclear weapons. We dedicate our most sophisticated science to the fashioning of new instruments of war. We burden our economy and overtax ourselves in the mass production of weapons.

We prepare for a war we know to be our doom. For we know that a nuclear war will be lethal beyond belief. Specialists in weaponry, aided by banks of computers, thumb through neat stacks of computer printouts careless of the fact that few men in the Northern Hemisphere will walk the earth in the aftermath of war. Genghis Khan was a Lilliputian in the ways of mass destruction.

Modern man and the ancestral Neanderthal have a common bloodstream and endocrinal system. It contains the stuff of war. As Thornton Wilder wrote:

> War is in all of us and is a very natural phenomenon indeed. During the millions of years that certain mam-

1

mals developed into man, the aggressive instinct was of the greatest importance.

George Bernard Shaw observed that man's heart is in his weapons. In *Man and Superman* the Devil speaks:

> Have you walked up and down upon the earth lately? I have; and I have examined Man's wonderful inventions. And I tell you that in the arts of life man invents nothing, but in the arts of death he outdoes Nature herself . . . when he goes out to slay, he carries a marvel of mechanism that lets loose at the touch of his finger all the hidden molecular energies, and leaves the javelin, the arrow, the blowpipe of his fathers far behind.

Although Shaw had no inkling of what was brewing at the time, two of his contemporaries busied themselves with seemingly harmless calculations that were to transform the world of weaponry. In Switzerland an obscure patent clerk by the name of Albert Einstein stood at a high desk, shuffling his calculations on mass and energy between his patent papers. An equally obscure schoolteacher in Russia, Konstanin Eduardovitch Ziolkovsky, worked away at the equations of rocket flight. One August day in 1945 when Albert Einstein maneuvered his little sailboat to the shore of Lake Saranac, a reporter told him that Hiroshima had been destroyed by an atomic bomb. The saddened scientist, whose fertile brain had birthed the basic idea underpinning the weapon, shook his head slowly and muttered that the world was not yet ready for the bomb.

Ready or not, the nuclear weapon became a standard item in the arsenals of leading world powers. And, all too quickly, it was joined by the ballistic missile, a revolutionary development fully as epochal as that of atomic energy. Man's modern blowpipe became "a marvel of mechanism" capable of hurling incredibly explosive warheads halfway around the globe.

The acronym ICBM (intercontinental ballistic missile) entered our lexicon, the "C" being interpolated to keep the Pentagon's hardware separate from the corporate initials of the world's largest business machines firm. Another acronym followed and dreadfully complicated the whole business of calculating the "balance of terror"—to use Winston Churchill's phrase. It is MIRV, standing for multiple, independently targeted, reentry vehicle. The intercontinental blowpipe, instead of sending a single dart at one target, could now hurl three, six, or even a dozen warheads, each guided to its individual target.

Behind all three developments—the nuclear explosive, the ocean-spanning missile, and the computer-directed warhead—was the mind of the modern weapons maker. Although, as in the case of Einstein, a single brain functioned to disclose the basic concept of a military development, the latter was brought to fruition by the mass action of many brains, some of them exquisitely configured to persuade Nature that she must give up her most deeply held secrets. G. B. Shaw was correct, but not sufficiently cynical; man's heart *and his mind* are in his weapons. Our society's greatest pooling of brainpower, its most extravagant concert in research, and its largest mobilization of industry have been dedicated to making new weapons of war.

Somewhere along this road to destruction, man lost his way and let his steps be guided by the compass of technology. Whenever a new weapon possibility beckoned, society meekly moved in this direction, without questioning the consequences. The natural sciences, for so long supreme in the grandeur of their isolation, became the great dictators of weapons events.

All the while, the weapons themselves became more and more impersonal and detached from the human experience. The business of war became quite unmilitary. After all, what is military about pressing a button that unleashes a deadly hail of Hydra missiles, bringing darkness and death to millions? There can scarcely be much of valor in such a clinical operation.

Man must be the master of his weapons and of their development or they will shape his destiny. But we no longer match weapons with our opponents; we seek to acquire whatever Nature proffers. This point is illustrated by a burst of candor that occurred when the Pentagon's director of research and engineering, Dr. John S. Foster, Jr., was testifying before a Senate hearing, presided over by Senator John Stennis ("Status of U.S. Strategic Power," Part I, p. 112, 1968):

> Now most of the action the United States takes in the area of research and development has to do with one or two types of activities.
>
> Either we see from the field of science and technology some new possibilities, which we think we ought to exploit, or we see threats on the horizon, possible threats, usually not something the enemy has done but something we have thought ourselves that he might do, we must therefore be prepared for. These are the two forces that tend to drive our research and development activities.

Here we have a prescription for a runaway arms race.

Given Dr. Foster's rationale for research and development, only a budgetary brake can slow down this self-directing juggernaut. But such restraints cannot be applied judiciously unless those in policy-making positions have a good understanding of modern science and technology.

The U.S. democratic system has depended on the traditional wisdom of the Congress to impose a set of checks and balances on the Military Establishment. Unfortunately, this countervailing force is now disturbed by ignorance and self-interest. Very few of our legislators have the kind of technical competence needed to judge modern weapons systems; moreover, it is rarely found in the committee staffs. In addition, defense politics enters into the funding of arms programs in that the Pentagon and industry conspire to promote weapons systems by bringing defense business to the political backyard of the key Congressional committee leaders.

President Eisenhower was right—there *is* a military-industrial (and political) complex.

Historians will record that the years of the Johnson administration brought defense affluence in large measure to LBJ's home state of Texas. Defense Department prime contracts awarded to Texas quadrupled during Johnson's term of office. During LBJ's last year in the White House the Dallas-Fort Worth area received $2.8 billion in prime military contracts. Ling-Temco-Vought (L-T-V), a firm headquartered in Dallas, had only $47 million in defense contracts and ranked sixty-first on the Pentagon's list of top contractors when Lyndon Johnson was Vice-President. In 1969 the firm's fortunes soared to embrace $914 million in defense business, putting it in seventh place on the Pentagon's list.

Considering the geopolitics of defense, it might be catastrophic if the United States were ever to elect a President from a small state like Rhode Island. No doubt the crisis of real estate would be solved by high-rise defense plants and assembly of rockets in a vertical mode.

If external checks and balances do not operate to arrest the dictates of our imperious technology, it is folly to believe that constraints will come from within the defense establishment. It is too much to expect of technicians that they will venture outside the confines of their specialties. Many of these men are of an engineering mentality, which is little educated to a sense of social responsibility. Furthermore, even the most enlightened scientists find it difficult to avoid being swept along by the momentum and enthusiasm of an urgent defense project with a fixed deadline.

I recall that during the summer of 1945, when the A-bomb was flexing the sheath of its technological cocoon, I collaborated with the late Leo Szilard, with whom I worked at the Chicago laboratory of the A-bomb project. The portly Hungarian physicist, who used to pace up and down the corridor of our guarded building in order to think through his brainstorms, knew that the A-bomb would be proof-tested in mid-July and would be used against Japan soon afterward. Szilard had played a key role in starting the U.S. atomic project; it was he who, together with a fellow Hungarian, Eugene P. Wigner of Princeton, persuaded Albert Einstein to write to President Roosevelt, asking that the United States begin work on a nuclear weapon.

It was natural for Szilard to feel a personal sense of responsibility toward the use to which this weapon would be put. One of his brainstorms was to draft a petition, which would be signed by project scientists, urging that the A-bomb not be dropped on Japanese cities but be used as a demonstration on a suitable military target.

Project Director Arthur Compton and I commuted between Chicago and the Los Alamos weapons laboratory, where the bomb was being assembled. I smuggled Szilard's petition into Los Alamos, but, to my dismay, I found that everyone was so busy rushing the weapon to completion that no one had time to think about anything else.

Atomic scientists exhibited a surge of conscience after Hiroshima, but with the passage of time their voices were less heard in the land. A not inconsiderable part of the scientific community adapted itself to the Pentagon's $8 billion per year funding of research and development. The corrupting influence of secret activities invaded the campus, creating pockets of the military-industrial complex in the university domain.

To the credit of the scientists, many survived the dollar assault of the Defense Department and retained their independence. They raised their voices in the winter of 1968-69 when the U.S. Army began to break ground for its antiballistic missile (ABM) installations in Seattle, Chicago, and Boston.

In a sense a handful of scientists conducted guerrilla warfare against the U.S. Army—a mode of attack for which even the years in Vietnam did not equip our generals with the expertise to counter effectively. It precipitated a great national debate over ABM and national security, a topic we shall consider at some length in later chapters. Suffice it to say at this point that the last common denominator in our democracy—the citizen—became concerned about nuclear-missile policy.

It is my contention that missile technology, not man, has dominated the evolution of our defense policy. I cannot recall a single research project of any size for which Congress refused to appropriate funds. Indeed, it force-fed a number of projects for which the Defense Department had little enthusiasm. Once an R&D project emerges from the conceptual stage and enters the development phase where big money is involved, then it tends to build up a momentum of its own. Then, as Senator J. W. Fulbright phrases it, the system may "soon acquire its own powerful constituency."

Nikita Khrushchev's Sputnik I, flashing through the October skies in 1957, set the United States on a crash course to outdo the Soviets in missilery. The U.S. reaction to the Soviet technological initiative turned out to be an overreaction, far outdistancing the Soviet ability to produce and deploy ICBMs.

Propelled by a highly advertised "missile gap" that became a political issue in the Nixon-Kennedy campaign of 1960, the United States pressed hard to develop and deploy huge liquid-fueled Atlas and Titan missiles. In addition, it accelerated the work on solid-fueled ballistic missiles such as the three-stage Minuteman and the two-stage Polaris, the latter to be fired from a submerged nuclear-powered submarine, acting as a mobile and concealed first stage.

The missile gap, as President Eisenhower predicted, turned out to be a fiction. As in the case of the "bomber gap," the Soviets failed to live up to their American press notices.

The Kennedy-exploited missile gap vanished in mid-1961, but it was a costly gambit, measured not so much in dollars as in terms of the step-up in the arms race that resulted. Kennedy's arms policy was sounded in a key paragraph of his inaugural address on January 21, 1961. Speaking on that bitterly cold day, when Washington was all but snowed under by a record-breaking storm, the youthful President proclaimed:

> We dare not tempt them with weakness. For only when our arms are sufficient beyond doubt can we be certain beyond doubt that they will never be employed.

Yet in his very next sentence, Kennedy warned about "the steady spread of the deadly atom" and "that uncertain balance of terror that stays the hand of mankind's final war."

"Arms beyond doubt" is elegant rhetoric, but in the nuclear-missile age, it could only mean that Nikita Khrushchev would be compelled to reciprocate and build up his own strike forces to match the U.S. kill-power.

Years later, when looking back at the course of missile policy, Kennedy's defense chief, Robert S. McNamara, was to philosophize about an "action-reaction" principle and to confess that we had probably built more missiles than we needed and had most likely forced the Soviets to do the same. President Kennedy had the opportunity, possibly a unique one in time, to lessen the tempo of the arms race.

Prior to JFK's election, the U.S. plan had been to build four hundred Minuteman ICBMs at a cost of $1.6 billion. Subsequently this number was doubled at a cost estimated to be $2.6 billion, and in 1962 the Kennedy administration added five hundred more Minuteman II missiles (later cut back to two hundred) and the total Minuteman deployment finally cost $11.3 billion. President Kennedy also ordered a speedup in the production of Polaris nuclear submarines so that from five deployed in 1961, the force jumped to twelve in 1963, to twenty-nine two years later, and finally to its present level of forty-one in 1967.

Many commentators endorse Kennedy's missile buildup as prudent national decision, pointing to the fact that at the time of the Cuban missile crisis in October, 1962, it was U.S. missile superiority that saved the day. It is certainly true that Khrushchev was outnumbered five to one during the Cuban crisis and that this disparity in missile strength was a factor in the Kremlin's decision to back down. But it was by no means the only factor.

We need to reassess the implications of the Cuban crisis and, particularly, to pay attention to the lesson President Kennedy said he learned at that time. The lesson, as related by Robert F. Kennedy in his *Thirteen Days: A Memoir of the Cuban Missile Crisis*, was "the importance of placing ourselves in the other country's shoes."

Robert Kennedy wrote that his brother-president was guided by reflection on how Khrushchev might interpret any action in the Cuban area and be forced, in turn, to escalate a response.

John Kenneth Galbraith, writing about the Cuban crisis, observed in 1969:

> I do not know what insanity caused the Soviets to send the missiles to Cuba—after showing commendable caution about the deployment of this gadgetry in far less dangerous locations.

One might add here that this was a caution not paralleled by the United States in placing Jupiter missiles on Turkish soil. To fully understand why Khrushchev acted so boldly in deploying Jupiter-like missiles in Cuba, we need to take President Kennedy's lesson seriously and apply it to the Soviet interpretation of our 1961 missile buildup decision.

On the basis of information released by the Defense Department, we now know the history of the deployment of Soviet ICBMs. We must assume that back in 1961 the Soviet planners had a reasonably good idea about the numbers of strategic missiles they would deploy each year.

Khrushchev must have known in 1961, as he pondered a response to Kennedy's initiative in the arms race, that he could not have a respectable strategic strike force deployed in the Soviet Union until 1966 at the earliest. Therefore, the Soviet leader would be condemned to playing second fiddle to Kennedy throughout the latter's full term of office, possibly even longer.

I believe that Khrushchev's decision to invest missiles in Cuba was not an insane gesture, but rather an act of political desperation, designed to offset the U.S. missile advantage in the early to mid sixties. Thus, John F. Kennedy may have induced the Cuban crisis by his missile decision.

The Soviets introduced a new dimension into the arms race in 1966, when they began deploying Galosh antiballistic missiles in a ring around Moscow. This was a Soviet initiative but the United States had long proclaimed it was about to deploy a missile defense of its cities. The U.S. response was not really in the action-reaction mode of Secretary McNamara, because no weapons systems today can be deployed without years of research and development having preceded such a decision.

The U.S. response was a decision to deploy ballistic missiles armed with multiple warheads—a fateful development that may well throw the arms race into an uncontrollable condition. The United States began development of a strategic system in 1962, designed to throw individually targeted reentry vehicles over intercontinental range. This

10

MIRV development multiplies a missile's warhead power manyfold.

By 1969 the Soviets had deployed sixty-seven Galosh missiles in the Moscow ring. The U.S. countermove was to equip its strategic missiles with MIRVs aboard Minuteman III and Poseidon sea-launched missiles. Over six thousand nuclear warheads were potentially added to the U.S. strike force, representing an overresponse that must inevitably trigger a new cycle of armaments in the Soviet Union.

This technological multiplication of the U.S. strategic forces came at a time when the two nations were drawing abreast of each other in numbers of deployed missiles. Thus it was that, when President Nixon took office, it seemed there might be some possible point of pause in the arms race—provided weapons technology could be kept under control. That would have meant getting together with the Soviets on a MIRV test ban. Instead, both nations persisted in their missile tests throughout 1969 and even as they talked at Helsinki.

Eight years after President Kennedy made his missile decisions that steamed up the missile race, President Nixon may well have made parallel decisions of even greater portent. One was kind of a nondecision, simply allowing MIRV technology to proceed without restraint. The other was a positive, but puzzling, decision on ballistic missile defense.

The Sentinel antiballistic missile system that Nixon inherited from Johnson had been fumbled by the U.S. Army, as scientist-critics quickly recognized, but some minor surgery could have healed public relations for this ailing ABM system. All that was required was for President Nixon to transplant the suburban missile sites to some farmland far from cities, and public turmoil would have been arrested. Instead, the White House ordered a wholesale review of the ABM issue, turning it over to Defense Secretary Melvin Laird, who promptly put his deputy, David Packard, in charge of the matter.

Even before the Laird-Packard team could report out its

recommendations on ABM, the U.S. Senate began an investigation of the Sentinel system. The great ABM debate of 1969, to which we shall give detailed attention, signaled a profound change in the mood of the Senate toward defense programs.

Apparently the early-warning political radars in the White House and the Pentagon failed to detect the signals emanating from the Foreign Relations Committee on Capitol Hill. Possibly, the White House and the Pentagon were alerted but dismissed the intent of the adversary as being unimportant because of an apparent lack of capability to win an engagement with the Administration.

The Pentagon obviously felt confident in its defenses against a Senate attack and for good reason. It could count on many senators to come to its rescue. Arms-oriented senators populate the critical Armed Services and Defense Appropriations committees, always ready to amplify any potential Soviet threat and to back any new defense appropriations. However, defense officials failed to appreciate the extent to which the credibility of the Military Establishment had been eroded by recent events.

Most of all, the baneful war in Vietnam with its lengthening casualty lists and its futility tended to undermine the authority of the military. The *Pueblo* affair off the coast of North Korea was a bitter pill for many Americans to swallow. Furthermore, a number of disclosures about the workings of the U.S. arms industry made Americans aware of the reality of a "military-industrial complex" and that it is capable of being a corruptive influence in our nation. The F-111 aircraft of General Dynamics continued to be controversial, especially after its military trials in Vietnam turned into a fiasco. The C-5A Galaxy—Lockheed's supertransport—attracted public attention after Air Force and company attempts to conceal cost overruns met with failure.

Military hardware, as the experts call the Pentagon's paraphernalia, had become so complex since the days of World War II that it seemed almost incomprehensible to the layman—and to the average senator. I rather imagine that some defense officials must have smirked at the thought of the Foreign Relations Committee taking on the ABM system as an object of scrutiny. Here the Pentagon failed to reckon with the impact that a hastily organized group of scientists could have on the ABM debate.

Then, too, the men in the Pentagon were probably overconfident, because they felt they could always resort to their ultimate weapon—secrecy. The Defense Department is long practiced in the fine art of the controlled release of information favorable to its cause. Its experts could always squelch a critic's voice by invoking a retreat to the sanctuary of classified data.

These two factors, secrecy and technicality, combined to give defense officials excellent armor against their critics.

At winter's end in 1969, the White House announced its decision on the ABM program through a nationally televised press conference. President Nixon made a flawless presentation of the program and unveiled his Safeguard program. The latter, which we shall examine later, represented still another swerve in defense policy on ABM. The new Safeguard system was based on the need to protect our Minuteman ICBM sites against a first strike by Soviet missiles. Missile saving, not people protection, became the support base for the new ballistic defense system. This abrupt switch in the ABM rationale invited examination and fueled the Senate debate on the issue.

Public examination of the Safeguard issue broke into the open the whole issue of nuclear policy. This was the great dividend of ABM debate. President Nixon had more or less invited such discussion, when he spoke of "nuclear sufficiency" in his first press conference in the White House. The following news items, taken from the Washington *Post* for

June 16, 1969, illustrates how one high-ranking defense official felt about this matter:

ARMS SUFFICIENCY DEFINED

Deputy Defense Secretary Packard shrugged his shoulders the other day when asked how much was enough in the way of armaments.

The President, he was reminded, had said that his goal was simply a "sufficiency" of arms. What did that mean?

"It means," said Packard, "that it's a good word to use in a speech. Beyond that it doesn't mean a God-damned thing."

Mr. Packard was, no doubt, reflecting the traditional view held in the Pentagon that arms supremacy should be the only acceptable military objective for the nation. Nuclear parity is a dirty word in defense circles.

The concept of sufficiency in arms is an anathema to the military-industrial-political complex, because it imposes limits on arms and thus on defense contracts. Arms contractors, fattened on the crisis years of the sixties, seek continued corporate growth through winning more prime military awards. Contracts are what make the complex click.

Vietnam caused defense funds to surge above the $80 billion annual level and aerospace firms, aware that a slump in the budget could produce a severe corporate setback, have prepared a "shopping list" of new hardware items that would bring in $100 billion in new defense business in the seventies. The Safeguard ABM is but one of the items the defense industry hopes will swell their fortunes. AMSA, the advanced manned strategic aircraft, a follow-on bomber to replace the B-52, is another big hope of the aerospace complex.

Defense experts like to cushion the shock of such big budgetary bites by expressing the total defense budget as a fraction of the Gross National Product, let's say as 9 percent of the GNP, for this is a figure that has applied during much of the sixties. Now that the GNP is lurking around $1,000 billion, these officials see no reason why the Pentagon can't get its 9 percent cut, i.e., $90 billion.

To agree to the Pentagon's claim on a fixed percentage of the Gross National Product is to indenture our economy to the military-industrial complex on a permanent basis. And, in the process, we would not only shortchange the domestic needs of this nation, we would find no net gain in our national security. We would be perpetuating an arms race beyond control.

It is the thesis of this book that the United States needs to make the most searching examination of its national security in the light of the new technologies of our time. I maintain that we have overreached ourselves in our quest for security and that by so doing we have led to an escalation of the arms race.

We have worshiped too long at the altar of our high technology.

II

A Modern Hydra

Hercules, the Greek hero-god, tested his might against the terrible nine-headed Hydra, a water serpent that terrorized anyone unlucky enough to venture near its swampy nest. Clouting its heads with a huge club, Hercules was astonished to see two new heads sprout where one had been before. He conquered this multiplication problem by seizing a burning timber and searing each head-stump until he came to the ninth and last head, the immortal one. This he cut off and disposed of by burying it under a rock.

It is no exaggeration to say that a technological Hydra has come forth to intimidate those who would attempt to control the nuclear-missile race. Weapons experts managed to re-design the nose cone of the original Polaris missile so that, instead of mounting a single warhead, it could be fitted with three separate warheads. These form a cluster or buckshot pattern around a central target. The U.S. Navy incorporated this multiple warhead in its Polaris A-3 missile which was deployed in nuclear submarine launchers during the late sixties. This development, known by the acronym MRV for multiple reentry vehicle, was kept highly secret so that it was not until 1969 that it became known that such MRVs were deployed aboard many Polaris submarines.

On January 18, 1965, President Johnson requested that the Congress approve funds for a further development of the multiple missile which the U.S. Navy called the Poseidon. It was estimated that some $800 million would be required to develop the new submarine-launched ballistic missiles and another $1.2 billion would be needed to produce them and to adapt the Polaris submarines to their increased size.

Defense Secretary Robert McNamara disclosed that the $2 billion price tag applied to a nineteen-boat force, that is, 304 Poseidon launchers. Testifying before a House Armed Services Committee hearing on February 23, 1965, McNamara spoke of the new program as follows:

> I inserted this in the budget, at the recommendation of the Navy and the Joint Chiefs, because we all believe that this is a major step forward in increasing accuracy and increasing payload. Both accuracy and payload increases will assist us in penetrating an antiballistic missile system if one should develop, because then we can trade off accuracy and decoys or other penetration aids. As of now we don't know whether an antiballistic missile system will be deployed.

Despite lack of intelligence about a Soviet ABM deployment, the defense secretary urged development and deployment of the weapons system, arguing: "This is, I believe, one of the situations in which we would be justified in coming to the decision to move ahead with the development as a prudent 'insurance' measure for our future deterrent capability."

There was no hint in the President's announcement of the Poseidon program, nor in his defense secretary's testimony, that the U.S. development involved fashioning the Polaris missile into a modern Hydra. The Navy selected from Greek mythology a missile name that was most appropriate, for

18

Poseidon was a god who could shake the earth far inland from his watery domain.

We now know that the Poseidon can carry up to fourteen individual warheads (MIRVs). Furthermore, as a response to the Soviet deployment of Galosh missiles around Moscow, the United States expanded the nineteen-boat Poseidon submarine force to a full thirty-one-boat level. The remaining ten Polaris submarines are too small to be refitted with the bulky Poseidon launch tubes.

The Navy's development program began in fiscal year 1965 with an expenditure of $10 million; this tripled the next year and then soared to $380 million in fiscal year (FY) 1967. During the next three years the Poseidon's development cost more than $400 million each year, so that by 1970 the total costs had escalated to $1.7 billion. Procurement costs had jumped to $2.1 billion and conversion of the submarines added another $2.4 billion, bringing the total weapons systems cost to $6.2 billion.

Thus the modification of the thirty-one boats in the forty-one-boat force amounted to as much as the original Polaris costs. But it would be myopic to focus on cost overruns. The real points to emphasize here are: first, that the U.S. response—we might call it, pre-response—to the Soviet ABM was disproportionate to the actual threat; second, the magnitude of the response was kept secret, so that in effect there was a hidden escalation of the arms race.

By the time that prominent members of Congress became concerned about Poseidon, the MIRV development was almost a *fait accompli*. For example, in the spring of 1969 Senator Edward W. Brooke (R.-Mass.) spoke out:

> A combination of political and technological developments has brought us to an unprecedented situation. It is now clear that the great powers will either devise ways of limiting the growth of nuclear arsenals or they will

19

plunge ahead into a costly and dangerous competition in strategic weapons with unforeseeable consequences for the peace and the stability of the world.

His concern for the mounting arms race caused the Massachusetts senator to introduce into the Senate a resolution urging a moratorium on MIRV tests. He hoped that, if the two great nuclear powers could agree not to test MIRVs, the technology of multiplying a missile's strike power could be arrested and it might be possible to arrive at some limitation of strategic arms. It will be recalled that the strategic arms limitation talks (SALT) were scheduled for the summer of 1969.

Unfortunately, when the U. S. Senate became worried about MIRV, the U.S. development of Poseidon and also of Minuteman III had already reached a point where the Soviets were justified in charging that the United States sought a MIRV test ban in order to freeze its technological advantage.

The first Minuteman III and Poseidon tests took place on August 16, 1968. According to the testimony of Dr. John S. Foster, Jr., both tests were successful.

The defense R&D chief concluded: "Our overall evaluation is that both Minuteman III and Poseidon have demonstrated feasibility adequately and we expect to meet our development goals. . . . Both programs will deploy on schedule."

It was late in the day, therefore, to consider arresting the Poseidon MIRV technology by means of a flight test moratorium. The U.S. Navy already had two nuclear submarines in dry dock, modifying them to receive the Poseidon missiles. The first Poseidon-equipped submarines were due to become operational in 1971 and the entire refitting of the thiry-one-boat force would be completed by 1975.

The MIRV situation with regard to the Minuteman was even more inimical to hopes for a test ban. Minuteman III, the MIRVed version of the U.S. land-based ICBM, had its conceptual origin early in the Kennedy administration. The following question-and-answer testimony which took place in the summer of 1968 reveals something about the U.S. weapons system that many Americans may be unaware of:

QUESTION (by Senator Mike Mansfield, D.-Mont.): *Is it not true that the U.S. response to the discovery that the Soviets had made an initial deployment of an ABM system around Moscow and possibly elsewhere was to develop the MIRV system for Minuteman and Polaris?*
ANSWER (by Dr. John S. Foster, Jr., director of defense research and engineering): Not entirely. The MIRV concept was originally generated to increase our targeting capability rather than to penetrate ABM defenses. In 1961-62 planning for targeting the Minuteman force it was found that the total number of aim points exceeded the number of Minuteman missiles. By splitting up the payload of a single missile (deleted) each (deleted) could be programmed (deleted) allowing us to cover these targets with (deleted) fewer missiles. (Deleted.) MIRV was originally born to implement the payload split-up (deleted). It was found that the previously generated MIRV concept could equally well be used against ABM (deleted).

Most senators believed that the purpose of the Minuteman ICBM force was to deter the outbreak of a nuclear war by making evident the U.S. capability to hurl ICBM warheads at Soviet cities and industrial complexes in a second or retaliatory strike. It was the threat of this nuclear destruction that formed the basis of U.S. deterrent doctrine to keep the Soviets from launching a first strike at the United States. Dr. Foster's candor raises grave doubts about the "targeting doctrine" of the U.S. Air Force.

It was not the first time that official statements had made observers wonder whether or not the U.S. strategic strike forces were not, in fact, primed to strike at Soviet missile sites rather than Soviet cities. Minuteman II, for example, was first deployed in 1965 and the Air Force claimed for it that the new missile carried twice the payload and had twice the accuracy of Minuteman I. The combination of greater explosiveness and accuracy was said to mean an eightfold increase in effectiveness.

Since the accuracy (usually measured as circular error probability or CEP, being the radius of a circle within which 50 percent of the missiles impact) was already trending downward below one mile, the eightfold increase in weapon effectiveness could hardly apply to large Soviet cities. Their lateral spread is far more than one mile. One could conclude that U. S. strategic experts were targeting "hard sites" or missile silos in the Soviet Union. It certainly would not be a farfetched conclusion to a Soviet analyst. This is a point to which we will return later.

Meanwhile, in the secret confines of Pentagon research centers the quest for more lethal firepower went on, being illuminated occasionally by technical outcroppings in the trade press.

For example, *Missiles and Rockets* ran an item in its August 23, 1965, issue, reporting that the Air Force had awarded a contract to the Autonetics Division of North American Aviation to develop a maneuverable reentry vehicle for Minuteman II. This system would supply "attitude and velocity control for the vehicle" during the post-boost phase of the missile flight. What was more than speculated about in this report was fully substantiated on December 13, 1967, when Dr. John S. Foster, Jr., delivered a speech at the Sheraton-Dallas Hotel in Dallas, Texas.

Dr. Foster began his speech by asking, "By what mechanisms does our society select the goals and opportunities which our research and development community will pursue?" He went on to explain that "many are pursued because they are possible or because they are exciting." I suspect that these lines provide unintended insight into the workings of the Pentagon mind. He then described MIRV as follows:

> That stands for Multiple Independently Targeted Reentry Vehicle, for those of you who love acronyms. For the others and for tonight let's just call it the Space Bus, because the payload is a space bus which contains many individual reentry vehicles with thermonuclear warheads. After the main booster has cut off, the bus keeps making minute adjustments to its speed and direction and after each adjustment it ejects another warhead. Thus each warhead is delivered on a trajectory to a different city, or if desired, all can be delivered within one city.

Thus after years of secrecy the MIRV Hydra was officially admitted. But essential details of Minuteman III and Poseidon were kept highly secret. Nonetheless, by piecing together bits of data appearing in Congressional testimony, in speeches by Pentagon officials, and by using some elementary principles of science, one can arrive at some reasonably accurate values for how many warheads of what power can be accommodated by the throw power of various missiles.

Minuteman III, for instance, is expected to throw three warheads over a range of five thousand miles with an accuracy of one-quarter mile. Each of the individual MIRV warheads has the power of more than ten times that of the bomb that destroyed Hiroshima. Because it throws its warheads over a shorter range of up to twenty-eight hundred miles, Poseidon can mount a greater multiplicity of warheads. The maximum number is fourteen but the average number is less than ten because of the requirement to carry penetration aids, i.e., devices like decoys designed to aid the warhead in penetrating the defense. Anything added to the throw weight of the missiles subtracts from its kill power. Therefore the Poseidon warheads average about twice the explosive power of the Hiroshima bomb.

Half the entire Minuteman force is expected to be MIRVed in the early 1970s and the Soviets must assume that by 1975 every silo hole will contain a MIRVed Minuteman III. Thus the Soviets must assume that by the middle of the next decade the United States will have a Minuteman force capable of throwing three thousand warheads at them. This is a minimum number because if U. S. experts wish to use MIRVs of lower power they can put half a dozen warheads in each Minuteman. This would add up to a strike force of six thousand warheads.

If we credit Greek mythology with prescience and take nine as the average number of warheads for Poseidon, then the thirty-one-boat force would mount a total of 4,428 MIRVs. Adding in 480 MRVs for the other ten Polaris submarines we get a total of nearly five thousand warheads throwable from submarines by 1975. The grand total of land- and sea-launched ballistic warheads is either eight thousand or eleven thousand depending on your assumptions. No matter how *you* look at it, the Soviet planners would have to make the worst assumptions and implement their own plans accordingly.

The growth of U.S. ballistic warhead power has been illustrated graphically in Appendix I for those who are log-arithmically minded. We see in this precipitous rise of U.S. strategic strength the true measure of the U.S. quest for security in the nuclear-missile age. The American penchant for winning any race, be it an athletic contest or an arms competition, underlies the ability of the arms supremacists who appeal to a patriotic fervor for being first. In such a competition it is easy to lose sight of reality—to relate the lethal power of the missiles to destruction of the enemy's resources.

Secretary McNamara became educated to the real might of the atom despite some of the academic mischief in which his "whiz kid" advisers often indulged in the Pentagon. McNa-

24

mara instructed his research chief, Dr. Foster, to keep him advised of U.S. strategic capability so that every three months he received a detailed report on how many casualties the U.S. strike forces could inflict on the Soviet Union and how much industrial damage would be sustained. This was presented in the form of a computer printout and was, of course, highly classified. As the years passed, McNamara clearly perceived that these grim statistics, the balance weights of strategic deterrence, needed to be given to the American people.

Robert McNamara, loyal to President Johnson, had endured the slings and arrows of misfortune, especially during his last year in the Pentagon. Saddened by the agony of Vietnam and unhappy about the prospects for coming to terms with the arms race, especially after having been forced to authorize a ballistic missile defense system, McNamara decided to inform the American people about the facts of life and death in the nuclear age.

This was not a sudden decision on his part. He had been wrestling with his conscience, as his 1967 speech in Montreal demonstrated; in it he forthrightly challenged the traditional view of numerical superiority in arms. McNamara asserted that more arms did not bring more security to an arming nation. His final statement on arms policy—and his attempt to bring Americans face to face with the essentials of the nuclear balance of terror—came in a 219-page document titled: "Statement of Secretary of Defense Robert S. McNamara before the Senate Armed Services Committee on the fiscal years 1969-73 Defense Program and the 1969 Defense Budget."

McNamara's swan song was not in epic prose but its message, often most brutally and cogently contained in statistical summaries, struck at the heart of U.S. weapons policy. Much to the surprise of Pentagon officials, material appeared in the document that had been previously held most secret. For example, the following table of damage data appeared on page 57 of McNamara's statement:

SOVIET POPULATION AND INDUSTRY DESTROYED
(Assumed 1972 Total Population of 247 Million; Urban
Population of 116 Million)

1 MT Equiv. Delivered Warheads	Total Population Fatalities		Industrial Capacity Destroyed (Percent)
	Millions	Percent	
100	37	15	59
200	52	21	72
400	74	30	76
800	96	39	77
1200	109	44	77
1600	116	47	77

This table was actually a summary of a computer printout of a detailed analysis of Soviet damage inflicted by a U.S. retaliatory strike. Actually the Soviet fatalities listed in the second column represent an underestimate of total deaths because they are calculated on the basis of death-within-twenty-four-hours, with no allowance being made for ramifying effects of nuclear damage.

The third row of figures in McNamara's table was underlined because "beyond 400 one-megaton equivalents optimally delivered, further increments would not meaningfully change the amount of damage inflicted because we would be bringing smaller and smaller cities under attack."

In revealing these grim statistics the Defense Secretary was incising the issue of nuclear deterrence with all the skill of a neurosurgeon applying his scalpel to a delicate operation. In the final analysis the Soviet decision to strike first at the United States would be determined by a careful assessment of how much damage would be inflicted on the Soviet homeland by the retaliatory fire of U.S. missiles.

McNamara admitted that no one outside the Kremlin's inner circle could know for certain how much damage the

Soviet leaders might accept as the penalty for initiating a nuclear war, but the death of seventy-four million Russians, the many millions of casualties, and 76 percent destruction of Soviet industrial capacity would surely come under the heading of "unacceptable" in any modern society.

In thinking about the "unacceptable"—as we view it—we must also consider how the Soviet planners would reckon "unacceptable" damage. It can be argued that the Soviet Union suffered twenty-two million fatalities in World War II and that it would be willing to accept a like number in its nuclear calculations. However, the Soviets did not make a conscious decision to accept such national injuries; in point of fact, they had little choice but to fight on or surrender. Futhermore, the damage was sustained over a period of years and not as a swift guillotinelike act of fury concentrated in a matter of hours at most.

Nuclear weapons make possible the massiveness of the national damage, but ballistic missiles compress the attack into a time span of minutes and hours. The criticality of the time element in nuclear war has not been sufficiently appreciated as a revolutionary change in the very nature of warfare.

Assuming that the Soviet planners manage to arrive at some level of acceptable damage, presumably much less than the four hundred figure stipulated by McNamara as unacceptable, their real problem remains—the calculus of a first strike and the damage represented by the return fire of U.S. missiles left untouched by the Soviet blitz.

The first strike must have a high probability of knocking out at least 95 percent of the retaliatory power of U.S. missiles while at the same time wiping out the U.S. aircraft capable of lugging nuclear weapons to Soviet targets. This calls for an exquisite, to my mind an impossible, sense of timing for the attack.

Insofar as possible a first strike must aim at prompt prevention of any return fire; this means killing off Minuteman ICBMs buried beneath the earth in their reinforced concrete silos, knocking out the Poseidon-carrying nuclear submarines, destroying many hundreds of intercontinental bombers at their dispersed bases, and eliminating the nuclear attack planes based in Europe and on board U.S. carriers. Such a global strike calls for an attack so orchestrated as to strike at all targets simultaneously.

Even if such a synchronous first strike could be staged, the Soviet planners must reckon with a nightmarish probability, namely, that the United States will act on early warnings of such a blitz and launch its strategic missiles while Soviet ICBMs are in flight. Somewhere in the Stygian blackness of outer space the descending Soviet warheads would hurtle past the ascending U.S. missiles. In consequence the Soviet warheads would impact near "empty holes," destroying and filling with rubble the silos that once housed the U.S. Minutemen.

There is simply no way that a Soviet strategist can deal with this dilemma of "empty hole targeting." Military men are by nature taught to assume the worst about enemy intentions and capabilities, and, in the case of planning a first strike, the Soviets would have to assume that U.S. missiles would be fired on warning of attack.

On September 18, 1967, speaking before a meeting of editors and publishers in San Francisco, Secretary McNamara asked himself the question: "Can the Soviet Union, in the foreseeable future, acquire (such) a first-strike capability against the United States?" Then the master of the Pentagon answered: "It cannot because we are determined to remain fully alert, and we will never permit our own assured destruction capability to be at a point where a Soviet first-strike capability is even remotely feasible."

McNamara surveyed the U.S. arsenal of missiles and concluded: "Our current numerical superiority over the Soviet

28

Union in reliable, accurate, and effective warheads is both greater than we had originally planned, and is in fact more than we require."

This was tantamount to heresy at the top. It was a frank admission of overkill, a charge that the Pentagon had repeatedly denied.

"Soviet strategic planners undoubtedly reasoned that if our buildup were to continue at its accelerated pace," continued the Defense Secretary, "we might conceivably reach, in time, a credible first-strike capability against the Soviet Union."

Undoubtedly Mr. McNamara felt that his decision to level off the Minuteman force at 1,000 missiles and the Polaris force at 656 missiles, despite military and Congressional pressure to expand the forces, represented a rational deployment—a nuclear sufficiency.

General Curtis E. LeMay had urged production of eight hundred more Minutemen and the buildup of new bomber forces. But while McNamara was struggling to keep his generals in line, he authorized research and development programs on multiple warheads.

Soviet planners, looking at U.S. strategic forces, would be justified in thinking that, while the missiles leveled off at 1,710 launchers, this was a temporary plateau, soon to be raised by the expedient of multiplying warhead power through the MIRV development. Thus Soviet analysis of the U.S. strategic strike forces might be that they represented a continuous growth in strength as is indicated in the upper curve of Appendix I. In effect, the MIRV technology may be interpreted as constituting a hidden escalation of the arms race.

The bitter irony of this concealed escalation is that the Soviets knew about it, since technology on both sides of the Iron Curtain tends to converge to a common terminus in weapons, but the Senate Foreign Relations Committee and the American people were not aware of it.

By the time prominent U.S. senators recognized the significance of the MIRV development and considered the possibility of a test ban, Minuteman III and Poseidon were $2 billion items in the fiscal year 1970 budget. And Dr. John Foster, Jr., could tell a Senate Armed Services Committee:

> If one were to reach agreement in the near future to ban such a thing as MIRV, it presumably means that we would not complete the development of Poseidon and Minuteman III. I see no sufficiently serious reason to consider altering the programs that are presented.

Dr. Foster, a product of the Livermore Laboratory in California where nuclear weapons are developed, spoke like a dedicated weapons maker. Yet Dr. Foster was more than a weapons maker. He was also a policymaker and the man whom Defense Secretary Laird was to rely on to back his claims for a Soviet first-strike capability—a matter which we shall discuss in the next chapter. Dr. Foster's mission, as the Defense Department's director of research and engineering, was to supervise the development of new weapons, not to worry about their relation to the problem of arms control. But someone, somewhere, in our federal government should have been worrying about the impact of technological developments like MIRV on the problem of arms control.

In his indictment of the "military-industrial" complex President Eisenhower stressed the undue influence of the defense community in our national affairs, but, other than warning about it, he gave no specific recommendations for combating its influence.

Here we have an $80 billion business, a virtual government within a government and almost a law unto itself, racing madly to develop weapons systems with almost no countervailing force to offset the great power of the Pentagon.

It is true that under President Kennedy the U.S. Arms Control and Disarmament Agency came into being, but this microscopic additive to bureaucracy is a mini-David pitted against a colossal Goliath. When the chips were down the power of the Pentagon was overwhelming. If a weapons system *could* be made, then it *would* be made; such was the imperative of technology.

McNamara, the computer-conscious master of the Pentagon, spent seven years as Secretary of Defense determined to bring the vast empire under civilian control. His all-embracing mind penetrated into the decimal-point crevices of many weapons systems, but in the end he met defeat, not at the hands of the generals and admirals who resented him, but rather because he could not conquer technology.

He had assumed an awesome responsibility under President Kennedy, being the first Secretary of Defense to be confronted with the reality of the nuclear-missile era, and his brilliant mind quickly grasped the paradox of power. He knew that no matter how much strategic force, even measured in billions of tons of TNT equivalent, the United States could accumulate, this was no index of political power to be used in international crises.

Certainly, the confrontation with Russia at the time of the Cuban crisis made this thoughtful man conscious of the limitations of the atom as a force to apply in moments of crisis. Self-educated as to the true nature of the atom's role in strategic contests, McNamara realized that the world was headed for trouble unless some measure of control could be introduced into the scheme of things. Yet he was virtually alone in the vast labyrinth of the Pentagon in questing for peace; the business of the Defense Department was war and preparation for war—for fighting wars and winning them. A vast gulf opened up between the Defense Secretary and his Joint Chiefs of Staff.

McNamara understood that the real mission of the Pentagon was the deterrence of war. The Joint Chiefs of Staff were reluctant to accept such a novel definition of their role. This is illustrated by the testimony that General Earle G. Wheeler, chairman of the Joint Chiefs of Staff, gave to the Stennis Subcommittee of the Senate Armed Services Committee in the summer of 1968. General Wheeler stated:

> Our national security objective is "to preserve the United States as a free and independent nation, safeguarding its fundamental values, and to preserve its freedom to pursue its national objectives as the leading world power." From this we produce our basic military objective, to deter aggression at any level and, should deterrence fail, to terminate hostilities, in concert with our allies, under conditions of relative advantage while limiting damage to the United States and minimizing damage to the United States and allied interests.

Mr. McNamara and General Wheeler parted company at the point where the General qualifies his statement with the phrase *should deterrence fail*. It is precisely this difference that is not well understood by the general public. The mission of the Defense Department had undergone tremendous change since Hiroshima and Sputnik. In effect, defense of the home-land becomes impossible in the nuclear-missile age.

McNamara understood that a powerful offense could overwhelm any defense. This same conclusion had been reached shortly after Hiroshima—in fact, even before the first A-bomb was tested—by a small group of atomic scientists whose spiritual leader was Leo Szilard.

When the Hungarian scientist said, "There is no defense," he did not mean that there would never be a measure of defense. I recall that in some of our pre-Hiroshima after-hours conversations—times when Szilard would emerge from the elevator directly opposite my laboratory door and drop in for a chat—he spoke of much more powerful bombs and their vast destructiveness. Offense, he felt, would always keep two jumps ahead of defense. But the same technology that fostered ocean-spanning ICBMs of high accuracy fed back to the hardware of shorter range defensive weapons and raised the possibility that the defense equation, previously reckoned purely in terms of offensive missile power, would be modified.

This possibility—one that the U.S. Army concentrated on as we shall relate in the following chapter—in turn impelled those developing offensive hardware to look to their laurels and perfect even more potent instruments of attack. Thus it was that the single-warheaded ICBM, like the mythological Hydra, grew multiple warheads, stepping up the arms race at the very time when it appeared that the two nuclear giants might come to some limitation of strategic arms.

When the Defense Secretary, who ruled the Pentagon as ballistic missiles came to power, stepped down from his high office he had failed to stem the tide of the arms race. Despite his best intentions he found it necessary to authorize a vast expansion of strategic striking power, and he was forced by political circumstance to give the go-ahead to a huge ballistic missile defense program.

"There is a kind of mad momentum intrinsic to the development of all new nuclear weaponry," observed McNamara. "If a weapon system works—and works well—there is strong pressure from many directions to procure and deploy the weapon out of all proportion to the prudent level required."

This was a profoundly sad admission to come from a man who glorified analysis and who pinpointed it in these words: "The basic objective of the management system we are introducing and trying to operate is to establish a rational foundation as opposed to an emotional foundation for the decisions as to what size force and what type of force this country will maintain."

Twin forces prevailed to overcome the McNamara concept of weapon rationality. One, in the case of offensive missiles, was the "mad momentum" of which he spoke; the other, in the instance of the ballistic defense system, was political. Despite this double defeat McNamara did succeed in his personal campaign to translate the grisly facts of nuclear policy from the icy statistics of computer printout to comprehensible prose. This exposition of nuclear deterrence was fundamental to the national dialogue that ensued in 1969 when the U.S. Senate came to grips with decision-making on nuclear weapons.

III

Sentinel and Safeguard

The first major decision made by President Richard M. Nixon was one involving national defense and high technology. Earlier, President Johnson had succeeded in getting Congress to approve funds for his Sentinel System, a national antiballistic missile system designed primarily to fend off a light Chinese attack in the 1970s. However, many observers believe that President Johnson backed this ABM program as protection against political attack from the Republicans. Politicians know that it does not pay to appear on the political stump as being responsible for not doing everything possible to insure the nation's defense.

The Sentinel program was intensively debated by Congress before approving it in 1968, but when the U.S. Army, the party responsible for developing and deploying ABMs in the United States, began implementing the program, it made a bad mistake. Army officials selected ABM sites within metropolitan Seattle and Boston and also in the suburbs of Chicago. This was an avoidable blunder since the missiles purportedly being deployed at these sites were long-range Spartans that could be located far from the city.

It appeared to angry citizens in these three cities that the U.S. Army was jumping the gun and planning to do more than install Spartans; they felt shorter range Sprint missiles would be sited in these locations as part of a thick ABM system. The public furor over having uninvited "nuclear neighbors" was in full cry when President Nixon took office.

Rather than doctor up the ailing Sentinel System by pulling back the metropolitan missile sites to more remote and non-disturbing locations, Nixon authorized a wholesale restudy of the ABM System.

The result was not only a revamped system, named Safeguard, but also a shift in the support base for the program from defense of people to protection of Minuteman missile silos. This abrupt swerve in defense policy, coming after angry Congressional debate on the Sentinel system, precipitated a full-scale battle between forces in the U.S. Senate and within the Pentagon.

To understand why President Nixon ran into such bitter and prolonged opposition to this Safeguard program we need to backtrack and examine the evolution of ABM policy and weapons development. Our retroview of the ABM takes us back to the days of World War II when the U.S. Army began its research on ballistic defense.

On February 8, 1945, Army Ordnance CPFF Contract No. W30-069-ORD-3182 was given to the Bell Telephone Laboratories. This Western Electric facility was authorized to proceed with "investigations, research experiments, design, development, and engineering work required to produce a suitable antiaircraft missile." The U.S. Army did not see any intercontinental ballistic missile over the horizon, but it did project a need for defense of U.S. cities against bombers.

Western Electric, the manufacturing arm of American Telephone and Telegraph Company, still remains the prime contractor for the Army's ballistic program even after the passage of almost a quarter of a century. The work proceeded cautiously at first and without any great funding; the latter ran to about $3 million per year during the late 1940s. However, the advent of the atomic bomb made the Pentagon conscious of the vulnerability of American cities, and priority was attached to the development of Nike-Ajax, the first of the Army's fledglings.

Nike-Ajax, its stubby fins making it appear more fish than bird, seemed reluctant to leave its earth nest but finally, in November, 1951, it streaked into the skies over the White Sands Proving Ground in New Mexico and scored a hit on a drone aircraft.

This first-generation missile was boosted by a solid-fueled first stage and propelled up to fifteen hundred miles per hour by a liquid-fueled second stage. Its range was twenty-five miles, and it could soar to an altitude of twelve miles to explode its TNT warhead. Nike-Ajax was judged to be reliable and was deployed around U.S. cities and air bases as a bomber defense.

Army experts knew that there was no future in depending on short-range missile-interceptors armed with high explosives, so they set about developing a second-generation, longer range Nike. Five years were required to develop this nuclear-tipped Nike-Hercules. The seventy-five-mile range missile became operational in 1958, replacing the aging Ajax in some eighty antiaircraft batteries in the United States. Some three thousand Hercules missiles were produced to defend American cities against Soviet bombers.

Missile specialists who had their eyes on developing an interceptor to challenge an ICBM were inhibited because of the prevailing consensus that this was like hitting a bullet with a bullet, and it was therefore impossible. But in the mid-1950s, when the hydrogen bomb became a reality and endowed an intercontinental missile with immense destructive power, there was greater urgency for city defense and, at the same time, a sense of despair that such defense could ever be leakproof.

Nonetheless, in 1955 the Army began work on an ABM, a true antimissile missile, through a study at Bell Telephone Laboratories. The origin of the word antimissile is lost somewhere in recent history, probably in the dust of London when V-2s first crashed there in September of 1944.

The Army's ABM effort was given a considerable boost by Soviet accomplishments in rocketry during 1957. On August 26, 1957, the Soviet news agency Tass reported the successful test of "a very long range ballistic missile" identified as the TR-3. Within six weeks Sputnik I flashed through orbital space and the world plunged into the Space Age. The Army was not hesitant in capitalizing on this development.

On October 28, 1957, General Maxwell Taylor asserted, "We can see no reason why the country cannot have an antimissile defense for a price that is within reach." Conscious of the popular disbelief in ABM, General Taylor continued, "I am sure many of you have heard the statement that the dollar requirements for this kind of defense are astronomical and that the whole concept is beyond consideration. I can assure you that studies I have seen lead me to a different conclusion."

This turned out to be the opening round in a series of Army attempts to win public support for deployment of an ABM system.

When General Taylor made his pitch for a major Army project to defend America against the ballistic threat posed by the Soviet Union, he knew that a third generation antimissile, the Nike-Zeus, was under development. He also knew that the Defense Department had spent over $25 billion on air defense measures since the end of the war, and he reasoned that the nation should be able to afford at least an equal sum to protect itself against ICBMs.

It was not a clear field for the Army because the U.S. Air Force considered that missiles were its special domain, and it already had a Bomarc missile deployed in North America and had a new antimissile, the Wizard, under development.

This interservice rivalry for the ABM was resolved under

the Eisenhower administration when Defense Secretary Neil McElroy fired off a pair of directives on January 16, 1958, dividing up the ABM effort between the Army and Air Force, but clearly giving the former first rights.

Mr. McElroy also created a new agency, the Advanced Research Projects Agency (ARPA), as a high-level organization, part of whose responsibility would be to pursue Project Defender. The latter, funded at an average of $100 million per year for almost a decade, was the trailbreaker in the antimissile field, its emphasis being heavily oriented toward science as opposed to the Army's concentration on ABM technology.

Nike-Zeus, the Army's missile killer, became its bid for its share of the missile program. The Navy had its Polaris Program, the Air Force its string of Atlas-Titan-Minuteman missiles, but the Army had only a defensive missile on which to place its bets for being big in the missile business. Zeus funding amounted to a modest $12 million in fiscal year 1957, quadrupled the next year, and then soared to $210 million.

At this point in time, although Zeus was still two years away from flight testing, the Army tried a power play by asking for funds amounting to $400 million in 1960 in order to begin producing Nike-Zeus as part of a national defense system. Secretary McElroy promptly denied the request, but Congress crammed the funds into the budget anyway. Eisenhower's defense secretary did not budge and refused to spend the money.

The fatal flaw in the Nike-Zeus system in 1960 was not in its missile, but rather in its radar and electronics. The system depended on a Zeus Acquisition Radar (ZAR) which was mechanically slewed, a cumbersome arrangement that did not permit the radar to discriminate between real warheads and decoys. Furthermore, the system was easily overwhelmed or "saturated" by being confronted with too heavy a warhead threat. All in all, the Zeus system was like a near-blind giant; it couldn't kill what it could not see, and its vision was very faulty.

President Kennedy's science advisers had no trouble turning back the renewed Army efforts on Nike-Zeus. Every new president gets exposed to many projects previously vetoed by an earlier administration. In this case, President Kennedy said, in effect, "No, not now. Come back later when you have done more work."

ABM went back in the Army's R&D oven, and this time the heat was really turned up. Nike-Zeus, now almost as big as a Minuteman ICBM, was in the process of proof-testing. Late in 1961 the first testing achieved its set objective and, the next spring, the missile worked perfectly in the firing of all three stages.

Zeus was readied for an intercept test on July 19, 1962. Poised in its underground cell at Kwajalein Island in the Marshall chain southwest of Hawaii, it awaited the radar signal that would send it thundering aloft. Its target, an Atlas nose cone, would be fired from Vandenberg Air Force Base on the California coast down a "threat corridor" five thousand miles in length. The island-based interceptor would at last be asked to live up to the heroics of its namesake, the god Zeus.

The Atlas ICBM fired on schedule and lobbed its massive dummy warhead straight down the corridor. Sensitive radars picked up the "hostile object" as it hurtled earthward on its downward arc. Signals beamed out from Kwajalein reflected off the dummy warhead and bounced back to the Zeus control point, allowing computers to fix its trajectory and to calculate the precise moment of firing the Zeus so that it could be guided to a mathematically determined intercept point in space.

Its first stage ignited with a roar and the mighty rocket zoomed upward, discarding the booster stage and streaking onward ever faster as its second-stage thrust powered it toward point X. Obeying the radar instructions, Zeus followed an

40

exact program as it shucked off its second stage and zeroed in on the attacking object. A hit was scored.

Although there were some skeptics who downplayed the event as a "turkey shoot," claiming that it was not a real combat test but rather a controlled experiment in which the attack was known in advance, the Army experts were elated with their success.

Furthermore, a "nuclear event" took place in the same general area of the Pacific that added to their confidence in Zeus. Experts from the Atomic Energy Commission detonated a powerful nuclear warhead in space, some two hundred miles above Johnson Island. The two-megaton warhead, possessing one hundred times the power of the Nagasaki bomb, illuminated the night sky over much of the Pacific. In fact, some six hundred miles away an enterprising photographer snapped a photo of Diamond Head bathed in the refulgence of the bomb.

Data gathered from this test convinced atomic scientists that an interceptor missile like Zeus could be armed with a potent means of killing off an incoming warhead. The basis for this optimism is to be found in analyzing the nature of a nuclear burst in space.

When a powerful nuclear weapon is exploded in the vacuum of space, it bears little resemblance to a detonation deep in the atmosphere. It is a strange explosion, almost incomprehensible to laymen accustomed to the fireball and fantastic blast of an air burst. When a nuclear explosion occurs in space, it produces very little direct light and no blast effect. In one-tenth of a millionth of a second the bomb's energy is emitted as a silent flicker of X rays and nuclear radiation.

Roughly eight-tenths of the energy comes off in the form of soft X rays, meaning the kind that is almost ten times weaker than the X rays used by a dentist. Although these are weak X rays, there is nothing in the emptiness of space to obstruct them so they flash out in all directions without losing energy.

Those striking the atmosphere get absorbed and have their energy converted into various forms of visible light. The X-ray kill of Spartan's warhead—the multimegaton explosive carried by the long-range U.S. interceptor missile—can extend over one thousand cubic miles of space. This corresponds to a lethal radius of more than six miles.

Should a hostile warhead encounter this burst of X rays one hundred miles or more above the earth's surface, depending on the proximity of the explosion, it could be disabled or destroyed. The X rays are absorbed in the outer covering of the hostile warhead and instantaneously convert this solid metal or ceramic coating (i.e., the ablative heat shield) into an ionized gas or plasma. This is called the fourth state of matter. Such an energy conversion can produce a violent shock wave in the warhead, disrupting its inner components just as certainly as if a charge of TNT had been detonated outside the bomb casing.

Alternatively, the X-ray impact may strip off enough of the ablative heat protection to cause the reentry vehicle to burn up as it courses down through the palpable atmosphere. In either event the X-ray kill can be effective out to a distance of many miles, depending on how the hostile warhead is constructed and protected. Thus it is not necessary for a bullet to hit a bullet in space if the missile kill is to be made.

However, the X-ray kill power of a Zeus warhead did not solve all of the Army's problems with the Zeus system. It was still necessary for the radars to track the incoming missile early in its trajectory and to identify it as the "real thing."

Failure to discriminate between the real thing and the phony warhead or decoy would mean that a Zeus warhead would be wasted or, given the confusion of many objects in the same area, would not know where to head. A resourceful attacker, knowing the Zeus capability, would be sure to devise ways around such a line of defense. Therefore, the Army reshuffled its ABM program, coming up with a new name in the process—Nike-X.

Nike-X became the Army's bid for a national system of ABM defense, using a one-two punch to knock out incoming missiles. Zeus would be the long-range jab designed to make intercepts one hundred miles or more above the earth's surface. But for those warheads leaking through this first line of defense, the Army promoted its short-range Sprint missile. As enemy warheads and decoys penetrate the atmosphere, the lighter decoys encounter more resistance and are separated from the real thing, which, being heavy, descends more rapidly. Ground-based radars would sense this difference in descent and direct Sprint to go after the heavy warheads.

Thus the retarding effect of the earth's atmosphere would be used as a filter to discriminate between fake and true warheads. Zeus would, in this new scheme of things, be an area defense weapon, being deployed at widely separated sites to defend all of the United States, like a series of giant umbrellas held aloft as a protective shield. Sprint, on the other hand, is of such short range that it is called a point defense weapon. Sprint, by necessity, has to be physically close to the targets it is designed to protect.

The Army contract for developing the Sprint missile was awarded to Martin Marietta Corporation in March, 1963. Because this new missile would have to make its intercepts close to the ground, it was essential that it be thrust aloft by powerful boosters capable of giving it high acceleration.

A "pop-up" mechanism was perfected to eject the missile from its underground cell, this being accomplished by using a powerful gas-driven piston to propel the Sprint out of its hole. Once clear of the surface, the first stage ignites, driving Sprint upward to an altitude of ten miles in about the time it takes to read this paragraph.

One penalty the designers had to pay for this lightninglike

speed was that the Sprint payload had to be kept to a minimum. As a result the nuclear warhead is only a thousandth that of Spartan (the current name for the redesigned Zeus). But even this kiloton-class Sprint warhead packs a powerful punch, one quite different in kind from Spartan's.

Exploded in the earth's atmosphere, the Sprint warhead destroys incoming warheads by blast and radiation. The primary radiation killer for Sprint is not X rays but rather nuclear particles called neutrons. These neutrons, unlike soft X rays, penetrate a warhead easily, splitting uranium atoms inside and "cooking" its nuclear core.

This neutron cooking, and blast effect, can disable the incoming warhead. However, it should be mentioned that this would not be visible on the ground since the radar would show an object descending without providing information about its condition. This would mean that it might be necessary for the defender to send up another Sprint to be sure of making the intercept.

The decision times involved in Sprint point defense are very short, measured in a few seconds. Yet within this interval a vast amount of information has to be processed and instructions given to the Sprint. As a point defense system, Sprint would have to be deployed as a battery of tens of missiles to protect a single city. Furthermore, because of the vulnerability of the radars used to alert Spartan and to guide the ABMs, it would be necessary to deploy Sprints to protect these installations. Radar vulnerability may be said to be the Achilles' heel of an ABM system.

Reviewing the ABM situation as transformed to Nike-X, Defense Secretary McNamara looked back on Nike-Zeus and commented:

It is worth noting that had we produced and deployed the Nike-Zeus system proposed by the Army in 1959 at

an estimated cost of $13 to $14 billion, most of it would
have had to be torn out and replaced, almost before it
became operational, by the new missiles and radars of the
Nike-X system.

McNamara was not impressed with Nike-X, but his Joint
Chiefs of Staff backed the ABM system and they won support
on Capitol Hill. Congress voted funds for Nike-X in 1966
so that the production line could be readied to turn out the
hardware of the ABM system. McNamara would not
knuckle under to this end run and pressure, but events were
conspiring to bolster the Army's hopes. These were happen-
ings taking place behind the Iron Curtain, and they concerned
Soviet progress in the ABM field.

For many years arms-oriented Congressmen had been playing up Soviet developments in missile defense. In the summer
of 1962, on the occasion of his informal session with American
newspaper editors, Khrushchev had boasted quite vehemently
that Soviet antimissile missiles "could hit a fly in outer
space."

However, any tangible evidence of Soviet prowess in ABM
work was lacking until May, 1964, when a sixty-five-foot
cigar-shaped container was trundled across Moscow's Red
Square. This marked the bashful debut of the Soviet entry
in the ABM race—the Galosh missile, to use the NATO code
word assigned to it. Within two years U.S. orbiting cameras
photographed initial deployments of Galosh missiles around
Moscow.

Although the data gathered by U.S. spy satellites are most
highly classified, McNamara was sufficiently educated in the
ways of the Pentagon to know that means would be found
to leak the news of the Galosh deployment to the press.
Therefore, believing it better to seize the initiative, McNamara held a press conference at Johnson City, Texas, on No-

vember 10, 1966, and disclosed that the Soviets had begun circling Moscow with an ABM ring.

Early in 1967 the Joint Chiefs of Staff came up with a unanimous decision to deploy Nike-X on a two-step basis, called Posture A and Posture B. The first program would cost $9.9 billion and would provide protection for twenty-five cities. The second, costed at $19.4 billion, would extend ABM protection to twenty-five more cities and would add more Sprints to thicken the defense of the largest cities.

Senator Richard B. Russell, the venerable chairman of the Armed Services Committee, backed the Joint Chiefs, arguing that Posture A would save eighty million American lives.

"It seems to me that the objective in defense should be to prepare to save all that you can," he said, "even if you are unable to save everything and everyone."

Pointing to funds appropriated in 1966 that had not been used, Senator Russell urged that they be employed to get Nike-X started. The pressure grew and the heat was turned on McNamara; he needed an asbestos suit to survive the cross-fire aimed his way in the spring of 1967. He fell back on his beloved computer printouts to establish his case.

McNamara agreed that Nike-X might save eighty million lives or even ninety million, though the cost might pyramid to $40 billion. But cost was not McNamara's objection to deploying Nike-X.

"It is the virtual certainty," he asserted, "that the Soviets will act to maintain their deterrent which casts such grave doubts on the advisability of our deploying the Nike-X system for the protection of our cities against the heavy, sophisticated missile attack they could launch in the 1970s. In all probability all we would accomplish would be to increase greatly both their defense expenditures and ours without any gain in real security to either side."

McNamara then displayed the printout of computer studies as follows:

Number of Fatalities in an All-Out
Strategic Exchange (in millions)
(Assumes Soviet Reaction to U.S. ABM Deployment)

U.S. Programs	Soviets Strike First, U.S. Retaliates Fatalities		U.S. Strikes First, Soviets Retaliate Fatalities	
	U.S.	Soviet	U.S.	Soviet
Approved (no response)	120	120+	100	70
Posture A	120	120+	90	70
Posture B	120	120+	90	70

These megastatistics, set down in the neat rows and columns of almost clinical analysis, probably do not have maximum effect on the human mind. I suspect that the average person and senator, as well, cannot conceive of such wholesale carnage. Yet there could be no questioning the validity of the Pentagon's computer printout; the machines did not lie.

While the Defense Secretary was busy with his tables of megadeaths, he was taking his cue from the lesson that President Kennedy is reported to have learned from the Cuban missile crisis, namely, to anticipate how the enemy would react to any initiative on our part.

His tables showed that an ABM system designed to protect the American population against Soviet missile attack would disturb the deterrent balance, causing the Soviets to make more missiles in order to restore the balance in their favor, thus offsetting the effectiveness of Nike-X.

U.S. fatalities in a first strike at the Soviet Union would be somewhat lessened, as compared to those incurred by a Soviet first strike, because some Soviet firepower would be destroyed by the preemptive attack. The reason why the Soviets would suffer 70 million deaths if U.S. forces struck first, as compared to 120 million deaths if Russia struck first and the United States retaliated, is that much of the U.S. firepower (on a first strike) would be directed to knocking out missiles and not to destroying cities.

The three rows of numbers listed in the table correspond to strategic situations as follows:

Approved (no response) refers to the U.S. strategic posture as it existed when McNamara testified. It assumed that the Soviets made no response to this level of defense either in adding to its strategic offense or defense.

Posture A corresponds to an additional U.S. investment of $9.9 billion in defense. The Soviet response to this action is assumed to consist of adding MIRVs and penetration aids to the strike forces along with 100 mobile ICBMs. Such a reaction would restore Soviet offensive capability so that a first strike would kill 120 million Americans, i.e., restore Soviet kill power to the level existing before the U.S. strengthening of its defenses. It should be noted that the reason for 70 million Soviet fatalities when the U.S. strikes first, as opposed to 120 million when the Soviet Union strikes first, is that a U.S. first strike would focus on missile sites, not on population, as would a retaliatory strike.

Posture B involves a heavy U.S. defense deployment by the mid-seventies, amounting to $19.4 billion. The Soviet reaction to this strategic action is assumed to be a further increase of strike forces by bringing 550 mobile ICBMs into inventory.

In the spring of 1967 the Republican National Committee issued a red, white, and blue booklet of approximately fifty-five pages, titled, *Is LBJ Right?* The Republicans made it clear that their question was directed to President Johnson's failure to deploy Nike-X. This cast the ABM in political and quite partisan terms.

A prominent newspaper commentator observed that Nike-X was now oriented to defend against Republican-launched missiles. An issue already complicated by secrecy and complexity, as well as by uncertainty of performance and Soviet response, was now interwoven with threads of political coloration.

Sometime during the last weeks of summer in 1967 President Johnson made up his mind about ABM deployment, and Robert McNamara was duly informed.

As one of McNamara's associates later told me, McNamara "for the first time went against the numbers." As though to ease his conscience, McNamara was allowed to speak out frankly on the nuclear defense problem.

In his speech announcing what became known as the Sentinel ABM System, the Defense Secretary unburdened his soul and gave voice to his darkest thoughts about the nature of defense in the nuclear missile age. The speech proceeded until almost the last page to describe the inadequacies, even the irrationality, of investing faith along with dollars in defense against a strategic nuclear attack.

It was probably the most evangelical speech ever given by a defense secretary; only at the very end does one find an announcement of an ABM system. Then one discovers that it is primarily oriented toward defense against ICBMs launched from Red China.

Putting a Red Chinese base under the Sentinel system seemed farfetched to many observers. In a sense, since the threat was keyed to an irrational attack by Red China, this support base for Sentinel tended to undercut the whole concept of nuclear deterrence.

The U.S. threat to inflict unacceptable retaliatory damage on the Soviet Union was counted on to deter that country from launching a first strike against our nation, but apparently such a destructive U.S. response could not be relied upon to deter Red China. However, it should be realized that McNamara could not be forced to go against *all* the numbers in his computer studies. He could not approve Sentinel as a "thick" system designed to absorb a Soviet strategic blow because he had already published his frightening damage table (previously described), and he was boxed in at this juncture. By the same token he could not approve a "thin" system against the Soviet nuclear threat for the simple reason that even the most dim-witted critic would charge that such a thin shield made no sense whatsoever against a massive attack of the type that the Soviet Union could mount. Accordingly, an anti-Soviet ABM system could not be justified by McNamara, and he was forced to look beyond the Soviet Union at the threat potential of the other nuclear powers. Since neither Great Britain nor France qualified, only Red China remained.

A "thin" anti-Chinese Sentinel system met with downright disbelief on Capitol Hill. Senator Russell expressed his view in reply to a question put by a reporter from *Atlanta* magazine.

> QUESTION: "Senator Russell, this so-called 'thin' system is just a foot in the door to beginning construction on the full or heavy ABM system, isn't it?"
> ANSWER: "It's a base for a system throughout the whole nation. I didn't deceive anybody. When we brought it up, they tried to dress it up as being designed to protect us from China. But I stated very frankly on the floor of the Senate that I consider it the foundation of a complete antimissile system that would save at least eighty million Americans against any atomic attack, however drastic."

This was a most astonishing admission to come from the man who was chairman of the Senate Armed Services Committee, particularly that he should speak of deception, for in this case the deceivers could be none other than defense officials. Since the Defense Department is the instrument of national security on which citizens must rely, it should be a most serious matter when a major weapons system is promoted by the Pentagon on grounds that appear so unconvincing, in fact, deceiving, to the senator most responsible for national security.

This is another indication that the ABM issue is not an isolated one but is an outcropping of a much more general challenge to our democratic society, specifically, the ability of democracy to control its arms establishment.

In the case of the Sentinel system, Congress finally approved it a year after McNamara's decision. Viewed optimistically, McNamara could say that it was a drastically cut-back Nike-X system costing about $6 billion. Cost overruns would probably boost this figure above the $10 billion mark. Viewed pessimistically, however, it could be the beginning of a larger system costing $50 billion or more.

This ABM system which the United States began to deploy late in 1968 consisted of fourteen missile sites for Spartans— the extended range Nike-Zeus missiles. A total of fourteen Spartan sites were to be located in the United States with five key installations forming a necklace across the northernmost states. This chain of five special Sentinel sites would feature a PAR (Perimeter Acquisition Radar) to provide early detection and trajectory identification of any hostile objects coming across the Arctic region.

Unlike the old mechanically slewed radars, the PAR equipment incorporated a new principle, that of phased array radar, meaning that instead of mechanically directing the radar beam out into space, the beam was swept out by electronic means. The proposed PAR, housed in a massive building two hundred feet on each side and one hundred thirty feet in height, would peer out into space for a distance of some fifteen hundred miles in the case of the blunt-ended Soviet reentry vehicles of the type used throughout 1969.

The 116-foot-diameter radar antenna of PAR, operating on a relatively low radio frequency, was designed to track many objects simultaneously, this being an absolute necessity since U.S. defenses would have to be geared to the threat of a Soviet blitz. Information once acquired by PAR would be fed to a data processing center that forms a central computation facility aimed at predicting the trajectory of each incoming object so that the exact intercept point can be calculated.

The PAR operation is designed to alert the Sprint-Spartan missile sites and to provide their Missile Site Radars with trajectory information. A knockout of the PARs would force the Safeguard system to rely on MSR for acquisition of the trajectory, giving it much less time to perceive an attack and greatly complicating the decisions to launch interceptors.

As the hostile objects continue on their downward arc, they move into the sight range of MSR, which is also a phased-array device containing five thousand sensing elements. It is somewhat smaller than PAR and its lower section is buried in the earth to provide some protection against blast damage. But because of the necessity for making the protective covering transparent to high frequency radio waves, the installation cannot be fully hardened. MSR's range is several hundred miles, but it depends on PAR for early intelligence about the ballistic trajectories of the attack force.

The missile site radar may be said to be the heart of the ABM defense since it must perform many tasks at the same time. First, it must acquire the trajectory of the incoming missile warhead and watch it as it descends in the atmosphere. Its associated computers must measure the relative sink rate of any objects simultaneously descending so as to discriminate between the true warhead and any decoys. MSR must also have a kind of double vision, one for long-range direction of the Spartan missile and another for short-range guidance of Sprint.

Here it should be interpolated that the PAR-MSR-Spartan-Sprint combination—the four elements of Sentinel—never received operational testing prior to the 1967 decision to go ahead with the system.

In fact, the first MSR-directed intercept with a Spartan is scheduled for mid-1970, to be followed by a Sprint intercept late in 1970. The actual firing of interceptors at the Kwajalein Missile Range in the Pacific in order to knock out multiple attackers is slated for 1971.

The justification for "jumping the gun" by deploying an untested system was made on the basis of the long lead time

52

needed to produce the hardware, the radars, the computers, and the missiles, so as to put an ABM system in operation in the mid-seventies.

In addition to the five northern Sentinel sites, nine others were to be spread across the nation to provide a thin defense against nuclear attack. As we have already reported, trouble developed for the Sentinel system when the Army began moving into metropolitan areas to site its radars and missiles. The city siting of Sentinel installations gave rise to the suspicion that Senator Russell was right, after all, and that the Army was moving up its time schedule and preparing sites for a thick ABM system.

For example, in the Chicago area the citizens of Libertyville took strong exception to having a Spartan base in their backyard. Some atomic scientists from the AEC's Argonne National Laboratory took up the fight, and the Pentagon had to rush its top experts to the scene.

This took place in January, 1969, and the citizens' revolt against Sentinel spread to Seattle and Boston. The latter site turned out to be a turning point for Sentinel since its proximity to the Massachusetts Institute of Technology almost automatically involved MIT in the debate. More importantly, it also brought Senator Edward Kennedy into the ABM issue, thus insuring maximum political visibility for the public discussion of the issue.

The controversy embroiling Sentinel was not lost in the calculations of the White House, as pointed out at the beginning of this chapter. But few observers thought that President Nixon would go so far as to change the support base for a revamped ABM program. Yet on March 14, 1969, President Nixon held a press conference and presented a national television audience with the first look at his Safeguard system. He explained that Deputy Secretary of Defense David Packard had conducted a two-month review of the ABM problem and had come up with four options:

1. To proceed with a heavy defense aimed at protecting U.S. cities against massive attack. This would be a full Nike-X system.
2. To continue with the existing Sentinel system.
3. To modify Sentinel, not to provide a heavy defense of cities, but to protect Minuteman missile sites and afford small-scale population protection.
4. To cancel the Sentinel program and revert to research and development, with no deployment of any ABMs.

President Nixon eventually chose option number three and in explaining his choice stressed the fact that other ABM choices involved danger of escalating the arms race by provoking the Soviet into arms responses. The Safeguard System was claimed to be nonprovocative since its primary goal was to protect land-based missiles against a first strike.

The Safeguard System would consist of phased deployment of PARs, MSRs, Sprints, and Spartans—in other words, the same components of the Sentinel System. Phase I of the system would deploy Spartan and Sprint missiles, as well as two PARs and two MSRs, to protect the two hundred Minutemen at Malmstrom Air Force Base in Montana, and one hundred and fifty Minutemen at Grand Forks AFB in North Dakota. An "investment" cost of $2.1 billion would be involved in this phase of the Safeguard program.

Phase II of the Nixon program involved three options:

Option 2A Extension of ABM defense to protect two more Minuteman fields and add more Sprints to the Montana and North Dakota bases. In addition, ABM defenses would be deployed to protect the "National Command Authority," i.e., Washington, D.C. Investment cost: $1.3 billion.
Option 2B Deploy ABM sites at ten locations in the United States as shown in the map in Appendix II. This

54

option was tied to the development of a greater Soviet submarine threat against U.S. bombers.

Option 2C Similar to the ten-site deployment of Option 2B except that this would be in response to an increasing Chinese ICBM threat.

The total investment cost for the full system would be $6.6 billion for all twelve sites, rising to $7.1 billion if two more sites are located in Hawaii and Alaska. By May of 1969 it turned out that these costs did not include $2.5 billion for research and development or $1.2 billion for nuclear explosives. The Safeguard price tag then amounted to $10.8 billion with no allowance for price increases or cost overruns.

By 1969 the total cost of U.S. research and development on ballistic missile defense was approximately $5 billion. Together with the additional R&D for Safeguard this would mean an expenditure of $7.5 billion to perfect America's defense against nuclear attack. An almost equal amount would be required to produce and deploy a twelve-site system.

It was not the cost, however, that involved Safeguard in a wave of public controversy far greater than that attacking Sentinel; it was a combination of factors. The national mood was one of disenchantment with the military establishment. Senators were keenly aware of the domestic turmoil in the ghetto, on campus, and in poverty-ridden areas; distressed by repeated examples of excessive and ever-rising costs for military programs, they seized upon Safeguard as a weapons system to be given the most detailed scrutiny.

Since President Nixon and Secretary Laird announced Safeguard as a counter to a Soviet first strike, it was natural for the Senate critics to force defense officials to justify this latest swerve in policy on ABM. After all, what had happened to so drastically alter McNamara's analysis of the defense situation?

To answer this question we proceed now to appraise the great national debate that developed over Safeguard as the Senate argued the issue in 1969. For the first time in the nuclear-missile era, the Senate came to grips with modern technology and tried to apply its judgment to a complex defense issue.

IV

The ABM Debate

Senator J. W. Fulbright, a chief architect of the opposition to the Safeguard program, spearheaded discussion of the defense issue in the prolonged debate in 1969. During the course of a colloquy with the arms champion, Senator Henry Jackson, the chairman of the Foreign Relations Committee observed:

> The real point of the debate is not the ABM as such. The whole point of the debate is an effort on the part of some members of the Senate to reassert some control over the military department. The Senate is the only agency of the government that can do it.

In seeking to apply the traditional checks and balances of democracy to defense spending, senators on both sides of the aisle banded together in a single-purposed coalition. Its aim was to defeat the Safeguard program.

On August 6, the twenty-fourth anniversary of Hiroshima, the critical test of the Administration proposal came in the form of a vote on an amendment to the authorization bill. Republican Senator John Sherman Cooper of Kentucky and Democratic Senator Philip A. Hart of Michigan proposed an amendment prohibiting the deployment of the Safeguard

System. Voted down 51 to 49, the Cooper-Hart proposal could scarcely be labeled a defeat. The fact that almost half of the Senate voted against deployment of a major weapons system must be rated as a radical performance by the legislators.

For President Nixon the outcome of the Senate contest may well be a Cadmean victory. It will be recalled that Cadmus, a legendary Phoenician prince, slew a dragon and sowed its teeth like grains of wheat. Thereafter armed warriors sprang up from the ground and proceeded to slay each other. The close Senate vote must be reckoned as a decisive warning that the power of the Pentagon is circumscribed.

Though the debate over the ABM issue was symbolic of concern about the necessity for controlling defense spending, within itself the Senate examination of the Safeguard System soon expanded to include a study of the general problem of national security and strategic deterrence. This latter development was brought about by Defense Secretary Laird's specifications with respect to Soviet ballistic missile capability. Previously top secret data were declassified by the highest echelon in the Pentagon in order to buttress the Administration's case for Safeguard.

Providing details about Soviet strategic capability was one thing, but Secretary Laird ran into a hornet's nest when he went beyond the limit of pinpointing the technical data about the Soviet heavyweight ICBM—the SS-9—and specified their intent.

In response to a question put to him on March 21 by Senator Stuart Symington, Secretary Laird said, "With the large tonnage the Soviets have they are going for our missiles and they are going for a first-strike capability. There is no question about that."

Senator Fulbright had many questions about that. Over a period of weeks, he hammered away at Laird's contention and the embattled defense chief backed down from his assertion of intent and settled for further details about Soviet technical capability.

It was somehow ironic that the U.S. Defense Secretary should express such concern over a Soviet first-strike capability, considering that the United States possessed such capacity for so many years. Having trailed this country in strategic strength, the Soviet Union could be excused for concentrating on "catching up." However, Laird's thesis was that the Soviets were intent on building up a strategic apparatus to destroy the U.S. Minuteman force.

At first Mr. Laird's case for a Soviet first-strike capability was based on disclosing the number of Soviet ICBMs. These included the SS-9—the heavyweight of the Soviet missiles—and two others, the SS-11 and the SS-13. The SS-11 has been dubbed a "city-buster" by the Pentagon because of its poor guidance and comparatively small warhead in the one-megaton class. The SS-11, like the SS-9, is a liquid-fueled ICBM.

A more modern ICBM, comparable to Minuteman I, was first sighted by our orbital eyes in 1967. This SS-13 missile has a warhead smaller than the SS-11, but it is solid-fueled. It represents a Soviet technological lag of some six or seven years behind U.S. missilery. Defense officials express the view that it may be deployed as a mobile weapon. Altogether, the Pentagon estimated in mid-1969 that the Soviets had deployed some eight hundred small ICBMs.

The Pentagon built its case for a Soviet first-strike threat around the SS-9. This monstrous ICBM is a liquid-fueled missile capable of hurling a payload of more than ten tons at intercontinental range. Such a payload can accommodate a warhead of twenty to twenty-five megatons. A thousand times more powerful than the A-bomb that destroyed Nagasaki, this superwarhead would be capable of imposing great blast or overpressure on a very large area.

If we take an overpressure of six pounds per square inch, which is enough to do heavy damage to most urban structures and to produce more than a 50 percent fatality rate inside these buildings, the SS-9 warhead could spread its damage over 320 square miles. This corresponds to a radius of destruction of somewhat more than ten miles. Defense analysts classified the SS-9 as a city-strike weapon and they estimated that Soviet deployment, begun in 1966 and continued through 1967, would taper off in 1968. This projection assumed that the Soviets would by then feel they had enough of the big missiles to form a potent second-strike threat against U.S. metropolitan centers.

U.S. defense officials had at hand thick stacks of computer printouts, itemizing the mortalities, casualties, and physical damage from a wide variety of nuclear attacks on our cities. Roughly fifty million Americans live in ten metropolitan areas. Another thirty million concentrate in the next score of largest city complexes and an equal number reside in thirty more densely populated areas. Thus a total of 110 million people are exposed to the risk of nuclear attack on seventy urban complexes.

The massive population movement from farm to city has resulted in half of the United States living on considerably less than one percent of the nation's land area. This urban population is packed into cities larger than a third of a million residents. Some areas like Los Angeles are of megalopolis character, spreading out over one thousand square miles of land. Even a twenty-five-megaton bomb could not strike at such a target and "cover" the area with heavy damage. Thus some U.S. targets would require multiple strikes. But U.S. analysts believed that one hundred SS-9s delivered on target would constitute an assured second-strike capacity.

A Soviet strike force successfully attacking one hundred U.S. cities with SS-9 warheads could mean the death of eighty million Americans. In fact, the SS-9's power would overkill the smaller city targets. Allowing for launch failures and errors in guidance, U.S. experts felt that the Soviets would level off their production of SS-9s at the two hundred figure as constituting an adequate deterrent force. Indeed, during 1968 the deployment of SS-9s stopped, seeming to fulfill U.S. intelligence projections. But then production was resumed and, when Mr. Laird took office, he discovered that SS-9 deployment exceeded the two hundred mark.

When Laird and his deputy, David Packard, appeared before a Senate Foreign Relations subcommittee, headed by Senator Albert Gore, they focused on the SS-9 as the *élan vital* of Soviet strategic strength. In what seemed to me an unplanned and rather improvised manner, Laird and his associates—primarily Packard and Dr. John Foster, his research chief—took the security wraps off the SS-9.

We were told that the huge missile was capable of knocking out a Minuteman silo because of its combination of accuracy and warhead power. The Defense Department was unwilling to release secret data about the hardness of Minuteman missile sites, but Packard did release a chart showing the probability of destruction for a silo as related to missile accuracy. It was easy to deduce that the hardness of a Minuteman silo was such that it could withstand a blast overpressure of three hundred pounds per square inch. Such an overpressure would be produced by a single SS-9 warhead out to a distance of slightly more than one nautical mile from its point of impact. A five-megaton warhead would produce the same blast effect at a distance of 0.6 nautical miles.

This piece of data was important, if those of us outside the Pentagon were to make an independent judgment regarding Laird's arguments on the SS-9 as a first-strike weapon.

On March 19, 1969, defense officials appeared as witnesses before the Senate Armed Services Committee, chaired by Senator John C. Stennis. It was an executive session, meaning that Secretary Laird and his chairman of the Joint Chiefs of

Staff, General Earle G. Wheeler, could introduce classified data into their testimony and then delete it from the printed record of the hearings.

Page 147 of the hearings presents an exchange between Senator Edward W. Brooke and Secretary Laird on the subject of multiple warheads for the SS-9 missile. In response to a question, Laird replied:

> The Soviet Union has gone forward with the SS-9s and has tested them with (deleted) multiple warheads. (deleted)
>
> . . . . .

On March 20 Senator Stennis convened his committee in open session to which television cameras were admitted. It was an unusual opportunity for the nation's television viewers to peer inside the rarely open doors of the Armed Services Committee.

As it turned out, it was also the start of public inquiry not only into the ABM system but also into the larger issue of strategic nuclear policy. A statement by Packard presented the Administration's case for Safeguard as a protection of the U.S. deterrent—specifically the land-based Minuteman force.

"This country," he said, "must assure itself and any potential enemy that at least several hundred missiles out of the one thousand deployed will survive and strike back against enemy cities."

Such was the Pentagon's opening gambit in making its case for deployment of an ABM system.

Following the Senate Armed Services Committee's exposure to the glare of television lights, the center of the debate shifted to an open session of the Foreign Relations Committee, namely, the one we have already described in which Senator Fulbright challenged Secretary Laird on a Soviet first-strike intent and capability. The defense chief hedged in discussing the multiple warhead capability of the Soviet SS-9, but on the very next day Packard assigned a triple warhead to the Soviet missile.

Each of the SS-9's three warheads was rated as being equal to five megatons in power. Data that had previously appeared as (deleted) items in Congressional testimony were suddenly out in the open. This meant that those of us on the "outside" could piece the data together and make independent analyses. Thus the "outsiders" could second-think the "insiders" and bring the issue to the forefront of public discussion.

Even before the Nixon Administration had recast the Sentinel System, independent scientists had turned their attention to analyzing the entire ABM issue. For myself, I had taken the subject seriously in November of 1966, when Defense Secretary McNamara made his announcement about the Soviet deployment of ABMs around Moscow. I felt that the ABM fat was now going to sizzle in the defense fire and that I had better be prepared to make a detailed study of ballistic missile defense.

I had for many years followed the practice of studying and indexing the voluminous Senate and House hearings on defense appropriations, preparedness, and military posture. This is quite a chore since the House hearings on defense appropriations alone may run to forty-four hundred pages of fine print. But such documents form a vital source of defense information even if they are often speckled with (deleted) parentheses.

The impact of the Senate ABM hearings in 1969 was to fill in many of the deletions—putting the outsider on more even terms with the experts inside the Pentagon. Fortunately some ex-insiders like Dr. George Rathjens and Dr. Jerome B. Wiesner, both faculty members at the Massachusetts Institute of Technology, threw themselves into the ABM debate. Thus the insiders were subjected to even more accurate fire from the outside.

The scientist-critics performed a valuable advisory role in

the ABM debate, but the senators themselves deserve the real credit for tackling a tough technical issue. When Senator Fulbright decided to pit his Foreign Relations Committee against the Senate Armed Services Committee, he was taking on a task of unprecedented magnitude. Senator Albert Gore, who chaired the subcommittee on Internal Organization and Disarmament Affairs, was not a stranger to atomic affairs since he had been a member of the Joint Committee on Atomic Energy for many years. But it was certainly an innovation for the Foreign Relations Committee to challenge the authority of the Armed Services Committee.

Senator Stuart Symington provided the Gore subcommittee with a vast fund of technical and military knowledge. As a former Secretary of the Air Force, Senator Symington had impeccable credentials. Furthermore, his views carried great weight with other members of the Senate.

In one of his many exchanges with defense officials during the course of the Senate hearings, he scored a direct hit on the Pentagon. His question went directly to the heart of deterrent doctrine. Senator Symington asked whether or not it was Defense Department policy to launch Minuteman missiles on radar warning of an impending attack.

The launch-on-warning drew an anguished response from Defense Secretary Laird. Yet the question was of cardinal significance to a first strike. Soviet experts planning a first strike would be schooled in assuming the worst. That, after all, is in the military tradition.

In targeting one thousand Minuteman missiles, the Soviet planners would have to assume that U.S. radars and other detection systems would pick up early warning of such a massive attack. Then, given this information, the U.S. decision-makers *might* decide to launch Minuteman retaliatory missiles *before* the Soviet warheads began impacting around the missile silos. It is true that U.S. leaders *might not* make such a decision, but Soviet planners could not count on it.

The big argument advanced to counter this launch-on-warning response to a Soviet first strike was that this was too risky a procedure—indeed, radars might give specious warning of an attack. Then the United States would be guilty of precipitating World War III without real provocation. But this argument was essentially rooted to the technology of the fifties when radars were prone to error. With this in mind, I proposed that the United States integrate its various early warning devices into a first-strike warning system.

My proposal for a first-strike warning system recognized that the United States already had two operational systems for detecting missiles in flight. One was the Ballistic Missile Early Warning System (BMEWS) that consisted of three gigantic radar installations at Clear, Alaska; Thule, Greenland; and Fylingsdales, England. These huge radars, 165 feet high and 400 feet long in antenna dimensions, could provide up to twenty minutes of advance warning of a missile attack. Built at a cost of more than $1 billion, the BMEWS radars were linked to the North American Air Defense Command (NORAD) by means of an elaborate $100 million communications system.

Linked to this system one could use the even earlier warning capacity of OTH—over-the-horizon radar. This OTH system was in limited operation in 1968 and reached full operation in 1969. The OTH radar depends on a backscatter of radiation emitted by overseas-based radar stations. Such a detection scheme can catch the Soviet missiles in the ascent phase and provide up to twenty-five minutes of warning.

An orbital system of launch detection using a number of satellites was first disclosed by the U.S. Air Force in 1969. Deployed in 1970, this orbital system is expected to be fully operational in 1971. It functions in the following fashion.

Satellites carrying sensors (i.e., sensitive detectors) look down toward earth and pick up evidence of missile launches, based on detecting the thermal or heat energy released by the combustion of propellants which thrust the missiles upward. Since much of the thrust occurs above the cloud layers, these orbital detectors cannot be blinded by bad weather. By detecting the exhaust emissions of ICBMs during the boost phase, these satellites could provide as much as thirty minutes of advance warning of a massive missile attack.

My proposal for a global first-strike warning system would integrate these three systems into a fully coordinated master system designed specifically to provide the United States with early warning of a Soviet first strike. In order to add insurance to this threefold system, I proposed in 1969 that a fourth component be added. This would consist of two "naked" PAR installations sited in North America, preferably in northern Canada, if such an arrangement could be reached. These Perimeter Acquisition Radars would be specifically designed to look out over fifteen hundred miles and track the trajectories of descending ICBMs. They would be "naked" in the sense that they would not be protected by Spartan or Sprint missiles. In other words, this detection system would not be part of an ABM system and would, therefore, be completely nonprovocative.

This four-tiered detection system would be hooked together as a global network to provide early warning of a first strike. Establishment and operation of this system would not have to be tied to a U.S. declaration that this nation would launch retaliatory missiles on warning. It would be sufficient to have the warning system in operation.

Its mere existence would serve as adequate notice to the Soviets that their first strike might well provoke retaliation prior to impact of ICBM warheads, leaving "empty holes" for targets. This would be the ultimate frustration for a strategic planner, but it would also serve as a persuasive deterrent to a first strike. The attacker could never be sure that his initial blitz would not see a reflex return fire of the very missiles he planned to destroy in their silos.

Assuming, however, that Soviet planners were not deterred by this great imponderable, could they hope to execute an attack so successfully that the U.S. return fire did not impose unacceptable damage on the Soviet homeland?

This question cannot be answered with true authority by U.S. experts since it involves substitution of American thinking for that of men in the Kremlin. But American defense officials must be rated as competent to answer the question of a U.S. first strike against the Soviet Union. In Senate testimony delivered in 1968 two U.S. authorities provided positive answers as follows:

General Earle G. Wheeler:
The Joint Chiefs of Staff have examined all types of preemptive attacks and first strikes and things of that kind, and we can find none that is attractive. In other words, the Soviet Union would still have the capability of inflicting very substantial damage on the United States.

Dr. John S. Foster, Jr.:
It is not possible today, nor is it likely to be in the future, for us to achieve sufficient strategic advantage over the Soviet Union that we could attack first and escape unacceptable damage in retaliation.

If the highest U.S. authorities maintain that a first strike is not feasible for the United States, how did it come about that in early 1969 Defense Secretary Laird could warn the country that the Soviets might possess such a capability in the mid-seventies? This was a question that baffled scientists and senators alike as they reviewed the defense data that became available by mid-1969. Was it possible that the Soviets had turned up a new weapons system that dissolved the integrity of the U.S. retaliatory power?

As we now know, the secret weapon of the Soviets turned

out to be the SS-9 heavyweight intercontinental missile. U.S. officials should not have been surprised at this development since Dr. Foster, himself, testified that this weapon was a reaction to a U.S. development.

"We have deployed a Titan I and then subsequently a Titan II in a hard silo," Dr. Foster stated. "The Soviet Union has followed with the deployment of, most recently, the (deleted) which is very similar to the Titan II." We now know, of course, that "SS-9" should be inserted in this sentence.

Dr. Foster expanded on the pattern of Soviet technical development and explained:

> So, in each case it seems to me the Soviet Union is following the U.S. lead and that the United States is not reacting to the Soviet actions. Our current effort to get a MIRV capability on our missiles is not reacting to a Soviet capability so much as it is moving ahead again to make sure that, whatever they do of the possible things that we imagine they might do, we will be prepared.

On this basis we should not have been surprised when the Soviets imitated the U.S. Titan missile. Our Titan I missiles were phased out by 1965 as being too expensive to maintain in operation and much inferior to the solid-fueled Minuteman ICBM. The fifty-four liquid-fueled Titan II missiles remaining in inventory were slated to be phased out as well, but were kept in operation on a contingency basis. Minuteman missiles were judged to be of high military value because of their reliability and quick response. Liquid-fueled ICBMs of the Titan class use storable liquid fuels that require complex pumps and plumbing.

Looking back on how the ABM debate developed in the spring of 1969, one realizes that political and defense leaders were poorly prepared to make a strong case for the ABM.

For one thing the sudden shift from a population-protecting Sentinel System to a missile-defending Safeguard System was so swift that it left many officials uninformed about the technical aspects of the new problem. Presumably, the Administration felt that it could rely on the traditional rubber-stamping of defense bills by an obedient Congress.

The big mistake that Secretary Laird made, however, was his failure to realize his new role as Pentagon chief was quite different from that of his former Congressional task of pressing authorities for more and more information. Accordingly, he proceeded to declassify certain defense data about the Soviet SS-9 and other missiles, thus specifying a strategic attack system to a degree that "outsiders" could make their private assessments of Soviet capability.

I know that personally I could scarcely believe my good luck. I found myself in possession of the same technical data that the Defense Department admitted it used to evaluate Soviet capability for a first strike.

To be sure all the essential data did not gush out at a single time, but gradually all relevant information saw the light of day. Therefore my calculations had to be revised as new data were released.

We can abridge our discussion of the controversy surrounding the SS-9 by jumping ahead in time to Secretary Laird's final presentation of the case for a Soviet first strike as presented in a letter dated July 1, 1969, addressed to Senator Fulbright:

1. The Soviet Union could acquire a capability to destroy virtually all of our Minuteman missiles. To be able to do so they would need:

(a) at least 420 SS-9s with three independently targeted reentry vehicles which have a capability of separating from one another by some relatively small number of miles;

(b) each of these reentry vehicles would have to have a warhead of approximately five megatons and a reasonably good accuracy;
(c) the SS-9s would have to be retargetable; and
(d) the range would have to be sufficient to reach all of the Minuteman silos.

Dr. Foster supplied data to fill in the qualitative remarks of his chief. He specified that the SS-9s would have a 20 percent failure rate, an accuracy of one-fourth of a mile, and an intelligence reporting system capable of signaling launch-control, if any of the warheads were not on course. Given these assumptions, Dr. Foster estimated that about 95 percent of the Minuteman silos would be destroyed.

Consider, then, precisely what the Pentagon was postulating for the SS-9 first strike. A launch-and-boost-phase failure rate for a mammoth liquid-fueled rocket of 20 percent might be attained for a test operation, but to assume that the Soviets could gear up 420 SS-9s to be launched as a salvo in two or three waves spaced minutes apart seems farfetched.

However, let us assume the Soviets are able to achieve such operational capability. Then they would presumably commit 350 of the SS-9s, mounting a total of 1,050 warheads, to the first salvo. Thus a net total of 840 warheads would be available for targeting 1,000 silos. Apparently Dr. Foster assumes this phase of the operation to be quite perfect, but I would have serious doubts about the ability of the Soviet rocket experts to dispatch their multiple warheads patterned to an accuracy of one-quarter mile.

Here we must mention a point of confusion about the nature of the Soviet triple warhead. U.S. Intelligence observations at the splashdown net in the Pacific where Soviet reentry vehicles are test-targeted have determined a triangular pattern for the shots. Note that Laird in his letter of July 1, 1969, to Senator Fulbright uses obfuscating language to describe the SS-9 multiple warhead.

It was not credited with a true MIRV capability, meaning that each warhead was not independently aimed, but was rather linked in a triangular pattern. This could be an extremely serious deficiency, since it would not qualify the system for attacking *all* Minuteman silos, but only those arranged in an appropriate triangular pattern. As we shall see, it would have even more serious deficiencies for the second and third follow-up salvos.

Even if each of the 840 separate Soviet warheads was a true MIRV and even if each followed an accurate trajectory to its aim point, this would leave 160 silos uncovered by the attack. But I would hasten to add that it is quite possible that a true MIRV system might suffer a variety of defects that would severely complicate an aggressor's problems.

First, the MIRV device might fail completely so that all three warheads—A, B, and C—were lost. Or it might dispatch warhead A, fail to aim B, and aim C on the borderline of the required quarter-mile accuracy. In such an eventuality the ground control would have to acquire this intelligence, relate it to similar information from the missiles in the first salvo, compute the retargeting necessary to strike at the "uncovered" silos, and then reprogram the backup SS-9s to dispatch their warheads to the designated aim points. All of this would have to be accomplished in a time measured in fractions of a minute.

The first striker must always worry about any broadening of the time span within which his warheads impact around the aim points. Once they impact, a reflex retaliation must be assumed. This means that there is a very stringent requirement for staging the attack as a simultaneous strike at *all* enemy missiles.

The attacker's problem in staging the follow-up strike to

hit at 160 silos would require committing almost all of the remaining 70 SS-9s with their 210 warheads. Since 42 would fail (based on the 20 percent failure factor), only 168 would be available for the attack.

An important consideration that must be kept in mind at this point is that this follow-up attack is quite different from the initial strike. The 1,000 Minuteman sites are dispersed in six fields consisting of wings of 150 and 200 missiles at sites in Montana, North and South Dakota, Wyoming, and Missouri. For example, each wing covers more than 10,000 square miles of area. In the case of the 200 Minuteman missiles at the Malmstrom Air Force Base in Montana, they are sited in clusters of irregular polygons with an east-west extension of 225 miles.

Suppose that the initial strike leaves thirty-five silos "uncovered." These will be distributed in a random and unpredictable pattern. To strike at them one would have to possess true MIRVs, not just the triple-pattern warheads, and one would also have to have MIRVs capable of hitting targets separated by considerable distances.

It should be stressed that an enemy first strike with ICBMs precludes the attacker's knowing for certain whether the warheads, thrown on what appeared to be a proper trajectory, actually reentered the atmosphere as planned, survived reentry, and detonated with full yield on impact. Here the attacker must depend wholly on his estimates; he has no way of getting direct damage evaluation from the target area. The military are accustomed to depending on visual or photographic inspection of target damage; this possibility is denied them when the attack is aimed at remote and hardened ICBM bases.

All in all, I found the Pentagon's case for the first-strike capability of the SS-9 most unconvincing. I made my own calculations based on a different assumption. I assumed that the Soviets would employ a true MIRV but that they would not depend on a system of follow-up strikes that relied on knowing which MIRVs had failed and which were on course. However, I was willing to credit the Soviet SS-9 with throwing more than three warheads.

There could be little doubt that the massive payload of the SS-9 could accommodate at least a dozen, even a score, of separate warheads. But multiplying the number of warheads divides the weight available for each nuclear explosive. In fact, it is not a case of simple division. One has to realize that splitting up the package into many smaller ones requires that allowance be made for propellant to guide this warhead and for the structure of the reentry vehicle with its individual heat shield. Splitting up the twenty-five-megaton single warhead into three parts reduces the total yield (explosiveness) of the three warheads to three times five, or fifteen megatons. A twelvefold split-up could involve reducing the separate MIRV warhead to half a megaton yield, depending on how the designers allocated their weight in the reentry vehicle.

Each of these smaller warheads would pack only a tenth of the lethal punch of the triple-headed SS-9 and they would, therefore, have to be more accurately delivered if they were to knock out a silo. By targeting half of the warheads at a single silo, an attacker could achieve a greater than 95 percent probability of knocking out the Minuteman inside. This would, however, carry no advantage over the system Secretary Laird and Dr. Foster attributed to the triple warhead for the SS-9. A single launch would not take out any more silos. But, as pointed out in Chapter Two, the multiplying effect of MIRV upsets the whole calculus of deterrence.

Despite the importance of MIRV, key senators masterminding the ABM opposition refused to bring this issue to the fore. It was introduced into the Safeguard debate as a side issue and one that would be dealt with later. But technology would not stand still even for the U.S. Senate and by the time some senators proposed a ban on MIRV tests both by the United

States and by the Soviet Union, the weapon had gone into the preproduction stage.

Had Secretary Laird played his cards more carefully in the instance of the SS-9, he might have disarmed his critics. Had he merely made qualitative statements about the multiple warhead capability of the SS-9 and left open the question of how many such missiles the Soviets might deploy by 1975, he could have made a less vulnerable case for Safeguard. He compounded this error by singling out the Minuteman force, as though it constituted the only element of the U.S. retaliatory strike force.

For example, just the strike power of the U.S. B-52 bomber force was enormous. The Strategic Air Command B-52s included thirteen squadrons (195 planes) of the C-F models and seventeen squadrons of the more modern B-52 G-H types. The latter are being equipped with SRAM, a short-range attack missile. SRAM development was begun in 1966 as a means of allowing the B-52s to overcome heavy terminal defense around enemy targets.

In addition to the B-52s, the Strategic Air Command has seventy-eight B-58 supersonic bombers and projects a total force of four FB-111 squadrons, each bomber being equipped with six SRAMs. As will be described later the SRAM is to be complemented with SCAD, a subsonic cruise armed decoy that uses electronic techniques to present a radar image identical to the bomber from which it is launched. The SCAD can be modified to have an MRV capability.

Adding up the U.S. bomber capability and that represented by the missile strike force, figuring in the nuclear-capable aircraft based in Europe, on carriers, and in submarines equipped with Polaris and Poseidon missiles, the total weight of nuclear weapons targetable by the United States was almost incredible.

As I listened to defense officials testify before the Senate committees investigating the ABM issue, I could not help but

74

recall that some nine years earlier I had been a witness before a House committee looking into the question of Minuteman missile siting. At the time I was shocked to hear General Curtis LeMay testify: "Higher levels of hardening will be introduced as required which will increase the number of enemy missiles required to between twenty and forty weapons for a single U.S. hardened missile site."

I countered by asserting that this would be true for missile accuracies in the early 1960 period but with the passage of time even the hardest missile site would become soft.

"Now, in the future," I testified, "one must expect that technology will be remorseless, that you will be going on and on and developing more and more precise missiles. I see no other way around this, and I believe that the development of precision ICBMs is an event which compares with the development of the A-bomb in terms of its technological significance."

In 1969 I found myself confronted with the significance of this prediction and, paradoxically, I was put in the position of defending the very Air Force policy I had attacked. This was not because of an incorrect prediction, but rather because of the unpersuasive way in which defense officials made their case for Minuteman vulnerability.

Secretary Laird addressed himself to the vulnerability of the B-52 strategic bombers in his letter of July 1, 1969, from which we have already quoted. In it he wrote:

> 2. The Soviet Union could acquire a capability to threaten severely the survival of our alert bombers. To do so they would need:
>
> (a) a force of about fifteen Y-class Polaris-type submarines on station off our shores; and
>
> (b) the ability to launch the missiles on a depressed trajectory.

It is significant that he made no mention of European-based

nuclear attack planes or of naval aircraft aboard carriers. Nor did he explain how Soviet submarines could launch their missiles against this far-flung network of nuclear attack planes in such a way as to deny other parts of the deterrent system warning of the attack.

So far as the submarine-based deterrent was concerned, Secretary Laird summed up his case in a third section of his letter to Senator Fulbright:

> 3. Although we confidently expect our Polaris/ Poseidon submarine to remain highly survivable through the early to mid-1970s, we cannot preclude the possibility that the Soviet Union in the next few years may devise some weapon, technique, or tactic which could critically increase the vulnerability of those submarines. Nor can we preclude the possibility that the Soviet Union might deploy a more extensive and effective ABM defense which could intercept a significant portion of the residual warheads. In any event, I believe it would be far too risky to rely upon only one of the three major elements of our strategic retaliatory forces for our deterrent.

In other words, Secretary Laird built his case for Safeguard by stacking one worst assumption upon another. The approach had been tried many times before and had usually worked. Congress had been only too willing to appropriate funds for new weapons systems. In the spring of 1969 the U.S. Senate for the first time in the postwar period subjected a major weapons system to a highly critical analysis.

In the foregoing we have treated the strategic threat to which the Safeguard System was proposed as a response. We must consider whether the proposed ABM system would be an effective response and, in addition, whether it would be provocative in escalating the arms race.

The essential elements of the Safeguard System have already

been described. Phase I would seek to provide a partial defense of two Minuteman fields in Montana and North Dakota. Since this was the part of the Safeguard program subject to authorization in 1969, we shall concentrate on it.

It is essentially a matter of "hard-point" defense. Since the long-range Spartan missiles must detonate their multimegaton warheads at least one hundred miles above the earth's surface, they can be deceived by the use of decoys that resemble the real warhead. The burden of hard-point defense must rest on short-range Sprint interceptors. These operate in a range from ten thousand feet above ground level to perhaps one hundred thousand feet. Radars can track the downward course of hostile objects and reject those from consideration which lag behind the most swiftly descending object, the latter being judged to be the real thing.

To deceive Sprint, the enemy could, of course, send heavy decoys along with his warheads, but this is a self-defeating tactic since it robs explosiveness from the nuclear warheads. But he has at his disposal a number of options. A straightforward alternative is simply to "override" the defense by throwing enough warheads at it to exhaust its firepower. This then becomes a contest between the number of offensive warheads versus available defensive missiles.

An attractive, low-cost alternative is to strike at the Achilles' heel of the Safeguard System, namely, its radar eyes. These can only be hardened to about one-tenth the level of the missile silos. They can, therefore, be attacked with small or relatively low-power warheads or with higher power warheads of less accuracy. Safeguard experts seek to counter this attack option by ringing the radars with ABMs. But this defense scheme can be countered through the exhaustion technique of showering down low-yield warheads or even clusters of heavy decoys. The SS-9 would be a potent means of doing this.

The whole business of missile defense is a kind of "cops and robbers" game in which the attackers may dream up innovations to outwit the defense. Since the Safeguard System will take until 1975 to become operational, it is clear that while it might conceivably work against modes of attack planned for in 1970, it might be rendered obsolete by the offensive technology of 1973.

The Pentagon's Advanced Research Projects Agency has for a number of years poured funds into ABRES—an advanced ballistic reentry systems study. Although highly secret, it is understood that one ARPA development stemming from ABRES is a technique for confusing an ABM defense by altering the ballistic trajectory of the U.S. warheads in their terminal phase. This departure from a rocket-like course or true ballistic trajectory can be accomplished by adding some sophistication to a MIRV. By giving it last-minute thrust, the MIRV can be shifted from its ballistic path so as to addle the brains of the ABM computers.

The Senate debate on Safeguard was inhibited by the fact that the Pentagon clamped a tight lid of secrecy on the number of missile interceptors to be deployed. So, in a sense, opponents and proponents of ABM were like fencers separated from each other by a thick plate of glass; they did not really engage. Since the effectiveness of the ABM defense hinged on one's assumptions about the nature of a future attack and since the Pentagon refused to specify its scenarios for a first strike, the debate meandered into an unresolved stalemate.

Scientists in opposition to Safeguard could charge that the Soviets could neutralize the effectiveness of the ABM system by simply adding more SS-9s to their attack force, the number amounting to some months of production. The officials supporting Safeguard invoked secret charts to substantiate their case. Senators were left to their own devices to judge which side was correct.

During the course of the Senate debate I spent relatively little time on the matter of Safeguard's effectiveness. My philosophy was that in this area the Pentagon held the highest cards. Moreover, the public was conditioned to believe that in technology anything was possible, provided you spent enough money on it.

In this connection, I realized that the cost factor was one close to the hearts of many senators, but I did not regard it as a critical one. My attitude was that, if the Soviets did pose a serious strategic threat to our deterrent and if the Safeguard System promised an effective counter to this threat, then the United States would probably be willing to foot the bill.

It seemed to me that the Nixon administration was too precipitous in proclaiming the Safeguard to be so essential to U.S. security. Had it prefaced this conclusion with an intensive and comprehensive assessment of the strategic situation, the case for Safeguard would have been more believable.

Furthermore, if the Defense Department had defined the various alternatives other than ABM defense, the case for the protection of Minuteman would have rung truer. Senator Albert Gore zeroed in on the truth of the matter when he asserted that the antiballistic missile system was "a weapons system in search of a mission."

The Defense Department had spent $5 billion on ABM research and development; it projected additional Safeguard R&D expenditures of $2.5 billion, not counting nuclear development costs borne by the Atomic Energy Commission. Here then was an $8 billion plus project seeking to be deployed. Defense-oriented senators could scarcely vote against any form of deployment without risking intense criticism of waste in the most costly weapons system ever undertaken by the Pentagon.

One of the most worrisome aspects of the Safeguard deployment is its long time-scale to become operational. It is not so much that this system may be rendered useless by new developments in offensive technology; it is that Safeguard is keyed to a long-term projection of Soviet capability. One can justify almost anything, if one projects far enough into the future.

Other defense options did not involve such long production and deployment times. For example, the national security would not have been compromised in the slightest if President Nixon had communicated with the Soviet leaders and warned that continued deployment of the SS-9 missile would be regarded as a provocative act, requiring a U.S. response. He could have warned that the United States would wait for a full year to perceive the buildup of Soviet strategic capability before ordering any response.

If the Soviets did continue the SS-9 deployment without letup, then after a year the President could have authorized any number of steps to be taken to offset the Soviet increase in strategic strength. For example, the Minuteman II production line is capable of turning out ICBMs in two years. Parallel site construction would allow these missiles to be deployed without loss of time. Thus if the President waited throughout 1970, he could still have more strategic offensive strength in place by 1973, two years before Safeguard would be operational.

Another alternative—and a truly nonprovocative one— would have been for the President to withhold deployment of Safeguard until research and development could bring forth a real hard-point defense system capable of protecting Minuteman silos.

The dangerous result of Safeguard deployment in its present form is that it is a makeshift system using the hardware of the old Sentinel System. This missile hardware is not identifiably a hard-point defense component. It is a carry-over from a system not designed to defend hardened silos.

"A good technical solution for this purpose," testified Dr. Wolfgang Panofsky, director for the Stanford Linear Accelerator Center, "should involve smaller and less expensive missiles and larger numbers of simpler hardened radars."

"If this hard-point defense is approved," asserted Senator George McGovern, "the Pentagon will then remind us that it is hopeless to try to defend even a compact ICBM site without increasing the number of ABM missiles and radars many times; they will tell us national security demands we triple or quadruple the size of our system. Next will come hard-point defense for all ICBM sites and SAC bases, and finally heavy defense for the cities."

Even if this prediction should not come about, the Soviets must plod the well-beaten military path of assuming the worst —that Safeguard will bloom into a city defense. Then they have no alternative but to increase their missile force in order to restore balance to their deterrent force.

Rear Admiral George H. Miller, director of the Navy's Strategic Offensive and Defensive Systems, testified early in 1969:

> The arms race is generated as you try to defend your weapons; as you put more defense and more hardness into your weapons, he builds more ICBMs, more throw weight to break through your defenses and break down your hardness. So it brings still more weapons toward the United States. This is a basic element of what is sometimes called the arms race.

To those of us who participated in advising senators during the spring and summer of 1969, it appeared that the Nixon administration did not make a strong case for its Safeguard proposal. Senator Fulbright summed it up succinctly and cogently in his reply to Secretary Laird's letter of July 1 to which repeated reference has been made. The following excerpts from Senator Fulbright's letter (as reprinted from the *Congressional Record* of August 5, 1969) illustrate the degree to which the senator comprehended the difficult technology of ABM defense:

81

The first of your three conclusions is that the Soviet Union could acquire a capability to destroy virtually all of our Minuteman missiles by the mid-1970's if they deployed at least 420 SS-9's with three independently targeted reentry vehicles and if certain other conditions were met with respect to warhead size, accuracy, range, and retargetability. Without recapitulating the technical objections that have been made by experts to this argument, I would simply point out again that your statement assumes that the United States would not deploy additional Minuteman missiles, or other appropriate weapons, if the SS-9 threat continues to develop. Your statement also assumes that the Soviets would not deploy more than 420 SS-9's, or additional smaller missiles to use against radar installations, if they wished to counter the Safeguard system.

The second conclusion is that the Soviet Union could acquire the capability to threaten the survival of our strategic bombers by the mid-1970's providing they have by that time a force of 15 Polaris-type submarines on station and the ability to launch missiles on depressed trajectory. There are, as you know, a number of ways to reduce the threat to our strategic bomber force. One is to disperse bombers, moving more bomber bases inland. A second is to renew the procedure of keeping a certain number of bombers on airborne alert. Finally, while you do not mention the fact, we all know that strategic bombers can be based abroad, so that Soviet submarines would have to be able to attack these bases as well.

Your third conclusion relates to the time period in which our Polaris/Poseidon submarines will remain effective. You state that "we confidently expect our Polaris/Poseidon submarines to remain highly survivable through the *early to mid*-1970's." Is it any wonder that the members of the Senate, not to mention the American people, find it difficult to take such a statement at face value when set against the statement made by Deputy Secretary of Defense Packard before the House Armed

82

Services Committee, on April 15, at which time he said: "Based on the data we now have, we expect the Polaris to remain highly survivable until *at least the late* 1970's * * * " Secretary Chafee, in a recent letter to Senator Gore, said that his views were in accord with Mr. Packard's statement. Other authorities have made similar statements. I note, incidentally, that while you refer to the agreement of the intelligence community with your first two conclusions, you do not mention the views of the intelligence community regarding your third conclusion. You simply refer to what, in your opinion, "cannot be precluded."

You also refer, in your third conclusion, to "the possibility that the Soviet Union might deploy a more extensive and effective ABM defense. * * * " Yet you do not mention the steps the Administration is ready to take, whether wisely or unwisely, to counter just such a Soviet development—that is, the conversion to the Poseidon system on our submarines, which will provide us with some 5,000 warheads instead of the 656 we now have, and the plans to fit Minuteman missiles with multiple-independently guided warheads.

I will close with two general comments.

First, by stating separately each of your three conclusions—that is, that the Soviet Union could acquire a capability to destroy virtually all of our missiles, to threaten the survivability of our bombers and to negate the effectiveness of our nuclear submarines—you imply that the Soviet Union could also acquire the capability to destroy all three elements of our deterrent concurrently. Many expert witnesses have pointed out in public Senate hearings that this implication—or perhaps it is an assumption on your part—is unfounded. If all three elements of our deterrent—that is, missiles, bombers and submarines—were not destroyed simultaneously, an attack on one would provide sufficient warning to permit use of at least one of the other two elements. Thus, a Soviet missile attack against our missiles would provide

ample time to permit our submarines and bombers to re-
taliate. Conversely, a Soviet submarine attack on our
bombers or our submarines would provide ample warning to permit us to launch our missiles. I will not belabor
the point but will add only that, while the intelligence
community, or the U.S. Intelligence Board, may agree
that the Soviet Union could acquire by some time in the
1970's two of the three capabilities you mention in your
letter, they have not agreed that the Soviet Union could
destroy all three elements of our nuclear deterrent force
simultaneously. Indeed, they have as you know, and as
the public record makes clear, never concluded that the
Soviets are "going for a first-strike capability."

My second general comment has to do with the assumption, which runs throughout your letter, that the
Soviets could achieve certain capabilities in the future
and that, before these capabilities are achieved, they
must be offset by our development of even greater capabilities. In making this assumption, you ignore the
mirror image that the Soviets must see, for on what
basis can we assume that the Soviets do not feel about our
development of greater weapons capabilities just as we
feel about theirs? Can they assume that we are not
intent on being able to pose the same threat to them
that the Administration says they could pose to us? You
have claimed in your public statements, for example, that
Safeguard will be an effective ABM defense able to intercept a significant number of their warheads. Yet you
state in your letter, as a justification for your judgment
that the Soviet Union could achieve a first-strike capability by the mid-1970's: "Nor can we preclude the
possibility that the Soviet Union might deploy a more
extensive and effective ABM defense which could intercept a significant portion of the residual warheads."
Why would our deployment of an ABM system, which
you and your associates claim to be effective, not be
interpreted by the Soviets in much the same way?

In sum, Mr. Secretary, I find, to return to your phrase,

that I too have a "problem of semantics." Mine arises in considering your contention that the deployment of the phase I of the Safeguard system would be "the most prudent and economical course we could pursue at this particular juncture." It strikes me, on the contrary, that the deployment of this dubious new weapons system, virtually certain as it would be to destabilize the present arms balance and to initiate a costly and futile intensification of the arms race, would be the antithesis of prudence, at best wasteful, more probably prodigal, and quite possibly disastrous.

Sincerely yours,

J. W. FULBRIGHT, *Chairman.*

In midsummer as the Safeguard issue drew close to a final decision, the battle lines were tightly drawn in the U.S. Senate. Although the White House claimed that it "had the votes," the opposition countered by stating that a nose count tallied fifty votes. Since the vote would come on the Cooper-Hart Amendment, fifty-one votes were required.

Two senators remained in the uncommitted column. One was Senator John J. Williams, a Republican four-termer from Delaware and a member of the Foreign Relations Committee. Insiders felt that he was most likely to vote for deployment of Safeguard. The other was Senator Clinton P. Anderson of New Mexico, a seventy-three-year-old former Secretary of Agriculture. Senator Anderson, a Democrat, was the one hope for defeating Safeguard, but I felt it was a faint hope since he was a long-standing chairman of the Joint Committee on Atomic Energy, a group noted for its hard-line defense views, and in addition his home state's biggest boon was the Los Alamos Scientific Laboratory, the major weapons design center of the nation.

The final vote, 51 to 49, on August 6, 1969, saw the Cooper-Hart Amendment defeated. On this roll call, Senator Margaret Chase Smith switched her vote which, on a previous amendment of her own, had been opposed to ABM deployment. In effect, it really was a 50-to-50 tie, lacking the necessary single vote for the amendment to pass. Both Senators Anderson and Williams voted for deployment as is seen in the following tabulation of the votes:

ABM Amendment Vote

DEMOCRATS FOR: 36

Bayh (Ind.)	McCarthy (Minn.)
Burdick (N.D.)	McGovern (S.D.)
Cannon (Nev.)	McIntyre (N.H.)
Church (Idaho)	Metcalf (Mont.)
Cranston (Calif.)	Mondale (Minn.)
Eagleton (Mo.)	Montoya (N.M.)
Ellender (La.)	Moss (Utah)
Fulbright (Ark.)	Muskie (Maine)
Gore (Tenn.)	Nelson (Wis.)
Gravel (Alaska)	Pell (R.I.)
Harris (Okla.)	Proxmire (Wis.)
Hart (Mich.)	Randolph (W. Va.)
Hartke (Ind.)	Ribicoff (Conn.)
Hughes (Iowa)	Symington (Mo.)
Inouye (Hawaii)	Tydings (Md.)
Kennedy (Mass.)	Williams (N.J.)
Magnuson (Wash.)	Yarborough (Tex.)
Mansfield (Mont.)	Young (Ohio)

REPUBLICANS FOR: 13

Aiken (Vt.)	Javits (N.Y.)
Brooke (Mass.)	Mathias (Md.)
Case (N.J.)	Pearson (Kan.)
Cook (Ky.)	Percy (Ill.)
Cooper (Ky.)	Saxbe (Ohio)
Goodell (N.Y.)	Schweiker (Pa.)
Hatfield (Ore.)	

DEMOCRATS AGAINST: 21

Allen (Ala.)
Anderson (N.M.)
Bible (Nev.)
Byrd (Va.)
Byrd (W. Va.)
Dodd (Conn.)
Eastland (Miss.)
Ervin (N.C.)
Holland (Fla.)
Hollings (S.C.)
Jackson (Wash.)

Jordan (N.C.)
Long (La.)
McClellan (Ark.)
McGee (Wyo.)
Pastore (R.I.)
Russell (Ga.)
Sparkman (Ala.)
Spong (Va.)
Stennis (Miss.)
Talmadge (Ga.)

REPUBLICANS AGAINST: 30

Allott (Colo.)
Baker (Tenn.)
Bellmon (Okla.)
Bennett (Utah)
Boggs (Del.)
Cotton (N.H.)
Curtis (Neb.)
Dirksen (Ill.)
Dole (Kan.)
Dominick (Colo.)
Fannin (Ariz.)
Fong (Hawaii)
Goldwater (Ariz.)
Griffin (Mich.)
Gurney (Fla.)

Hansen (Wyo.)
Hruska (Neb.)
Jordan (Idaho)
Miller (Iowa)
Mundt (S.D.)
Murphy (Calif.)
Packwood (Ore.)
Prouty (Vt.)
Scott (Pa.)
Stevens (Alaska)
Smith (Maine)
Thurmond (S.C.)
Tower (Tex.)
Williams (Del.)
Young (N.D.)

Seven of the nine senators on the Joint Committee on Atomic Energy and eleven of the eighteen members of the Armed Services Committee voted for deployment. But ten of the fifteen senators on the Foreign Relations Committee voted for the Cooper-Hart Amendment. The strongly conservative senators in the southern states gave their support to the President.

When the dust of battle settled on Capitol Hill, the victors knew that their narrow winning margin presaged a long-continuing argument over Safeguard and other major weapons systems. No longer would defense bills slide through the Senate with a minimum of debate. The Foreign Relations Committee had challenged the authority of the Armed Services Committee. Moreover, the victory for the Pentagon and the White House was not without its costs. Defense officials had released much classified information that would, in the future, form a weapon in the hands of the opposition. The Safeguard System would be periodically subjected to the most searching criticism.

Senators who opposed Safeguard and who pointed out its huge future costs would, no doubt, feel free to criticize the Nixon Administration at times of crisis on the home front. They could easily score by comparing the neglect of urban needs with the spending on missile defense.

The Defense Department suffered losses in the ABM battle that might have profound consequences for the future. In buttressing its case for Safeguard, the Pentagon exposed its whole deterrent structure to public view, revealing its potential weaknesses to everyone. The vulnerability of the Minuteman force was so stressed that its deterrent value was compromised for the future.

The Russians have a saying that a bear in the dark is always more dangerous than one in the open. Minuteman, veiled in secrecy, was more of a deterrent than when it was exposed in public debate. This might be viewed as an argument for keeping defense systems in the dark, but it is essential for a democracy to examine vital issues in an open manner. This is especially true when we realize that land-based ICBMs like Minuteman are the least amenable to arms control. If Minuteman is so vulnerable as to require its private ABM defense, then the United States should seriously consider scrapping these land-based missiles. The argument is reinforced, as we shall see, by the necessity for arm control.

At the core of the military desire to begin erecting the ballistic defenses of the U.S. homeland was a tardy realization that the advent of the nuclear-space age severely warped the old framework of the national defense mission—"to defend the United States against attack."

The military mission, stated in more modern form (General Wheeler's definition is given elsewhere in this book), emphasized deterrence of war. To the military mind nuclear deterrence meant nuclear weapon superiority. In 1969 it became starkly evident that mere numerical superiority in offensive missiles ceased to have its previous military significance. Given this new, near-equal balance in nuclear strength, American military leaders and their powerful spokesmen in the Congress sought a new measure of security in defensive arms.

This new quest for national security alarmed many a thoughtful senator and led to the unprecedented challenge of a major weapons system in 1969. "The path to that tragic new plateau of nuclear arms equilibrium," concluded New York's Senator Jacob Javits, "will be the most perilous mankind has yet trod in all history."

V

Scientists and Senators

One June night, when the ABM debate was in full swing, I stood behind the stage curtain of the Hollywood Palladium, waiting for Senator Joseph Tydings to finish his brief speech before an anti-ABM rally. We had just come from a press conference where senators, scientists, and stars mingled. Andy Williams, Candy Bergen, Henry Fonda, and Racquel Welch were among the stars.

Bill Cosby had "warmed up" the house, "winging it" as Carl Reiner remarked to me, and leaving the rest of us to wonder how we would follow his act.

"I first met the Bomb nineteen years ago," drawled Cosby. "I was in grade school." Then he proceeded to convulse the packed house with his description of a civil defense drill in his schoolroom. Meanwhile, I mentally raced through notes on my talk and decided to throw away the text and "wing it," too.

"I was introduced to the Bomb twenty-seven years ago," I began, thinking as I did so that it couldn't really be true. My thoughts went back to the wartime days of the University of Chicago campus where we struggled to birth the new weapon. Now, here I was, I reflected, speaking before a public rally, attempting to arrest a development that might send the arms race into a new and perhaps uncontrollable domain.

91

In the brief span of the postwar years, science had insinuated itself into almost every aspect of our national affairs. My workday begins with a reading of the *Congressional Record*, and it seems that I find something germane to science on most of the pages. This being the case, it was, I felt, important for Congress to have access to scientific advice of a completely independent nature.

To be sure, the various committees on Capitol Hill hear testimony from many scientists, but they are employees of government agencies. Every time a scientist from a federal agency testifies, he is subject to a double pull, one from his agency so that it will not be harmed by his statements, and one from the scientific community to which he is bound through the discipline of science, that requires the truth be told.

Unfortunately, the scientific community has very little organization and it has a tradition of not being political. Many professional societies exist, such as the American Physical Society and the American Chemical Society, but they prefer to remain aloof from politics. During the terrible days of the Oppenheimer affair, the professional societies sat on the sidelines and watched the battle rage.

Because scientists speak in a strange tongue and with many voices, it is difficult for Congress to bridge the science-political gap. My attention was drawn to the necessity for liaison between the scientists and politicians back in 1958, when it became apparent that the Eisenhower administration was not very much aware of the significance of science and technology as related to the nation's affairs.

I had enough political brains to realize it was the party out of power that most needed scientific and technical advice. So I sat down and typed out a letter to the Democratic National Committee, proposing that it establish an advisory committee on science and technology. It was surprisingly easy to persuade the politicians to venture into this new area—probably, I suspect, because Adlai Stevenson at that time was so influential in political affairs. In any event, the Democratic Advisory Council took the initiative of attaching to itself a group of seventeen distinguished scientists and engineers. Their activities were coordinated by Charles Tyroler II, a brilliant political scientist with whom I formed a lasting friendship and business association.

The fusion of scientists and politicians turned out to be a very fruitful relationship. Senators, big city mayors, governors, and Harry S Truman interacted with the scientists, and from this union there emerged some good ideas that could be converted into political realities. For example, the advisory scientists came up with the concept of a National Peace Agency as a positive force for promoting arms controls. Through a series of political actions, this concept was transformed into the political reality of the U.S. Arms Control and Disarmament Agency.

Many of us hoped that the new agency, set up under President Kennedy, would become a force to counteract the dominance of the Pentagon. However, it has remained a bashful chrysalis, reluctant to try its wings. In the case of both the Sentinel and Safeguard programs, the Arms Control Agency could have performed a great public service by making available a dispassionate White Paper on the subject of ballistic missile defense.

Other groups within the house of government could also have pitched in and promoted such a publication. For example, the President's Science Advisory Committee or the Office of Science and Technology could have authored an objective exposition of ABM systems. None was forthcoming. Accordingly, when President Nixon announced his Safeguard program, the Senate and the public had no authoritative document to which they could turn for assistance and elucidation of a complex technomilitary issue. All the cards were still in the Pentagon's deck.

One paragovernmental group, the National Academy of Sciences, should have responded to the nation's need for a White Paper on ABM. Established by an Act of Congress during Abraham Lincoln's term of office, the academy is the most illustrious organization of scientists in the United States. Its more than eight hundred members include the cream of the scientific society. Its charter calls for it to advise Congress, and it has done so on many occasions.

The precedent for promulgating a document to enlighten the public on a controversial technical issue was set in June, 1956. Then the academy published its report, "The Biological Effects of Atomic Radiation," as a means of clarifying the public befuddlement over fallout from bomb tests.

There can be no doubt that the public's concern and confusion on the ABM issue exceeded that of the radioactive fallout and test-ban issue. No technical matter ever received more front-page treatment in the newspapers and took up so many hours of television as did Sentinel and Safeguard. Why did not the National Academy of Sciences intervene and attempt to bring together the divergencies of the scientists?

This question is even more pertinent because, in the period following the fallout controversy, the academy took the initiative in 1962 of setting up a Committee on Science and Public Policy. This committee has three specific directives, one of which is spelled out as follows:

> As suggested from time to time by officials or agencies of the federal government, or as the need may be indicated by responsible expressions from the scientific community, the Committee initiates studies of problems of critical importance to science and to the nation, and publishes reports of these studies.

On the important issues of population and disposal of chemical warfare agents, COSPUP, as the committee is known, did a good job. Yet it failed to act on the ABM issue.

I think the reason for the National Academy's bashfulness in reporting on ABM is to be found in the top management of the organization. Dr. Frederick Seitz, who was president until July 1, 1969, also served as chairman of the Pentagon's Defense Science Board, the highest ranking advisory group on research and development.

Dr. Seitz made no secret of his views on ABM; in fact, he testified in favor of the Safeguard System before the Senate Armed Services Committee. His statement, indexed in the printed hearings under the heading President, National Academy of Sciences, wholeheartedly endorsed proceeding with the Safeguard development.

It is a matter of record that the august National Academy of Sciences refused to involve itself with a study on the ABM issue. This meant that the public was denied an authoritative analysis of the ballistic missile defense issue from an organization not charged with promotion of the Safeguard work.

Our democratic society lacks the mechanism for providing itself with disinterested analyses of military issues such as ABM defense. Effective criticism of defense projects is inhibited by the availability of information with which critics may assail the Defense Department's presentation of its case. The Pentagon can control the release of vital information in a manner favorable to itself. Furthermore, since defense projects are often critically dependent on intelligence, defense officials may obscure issues by releasing only certain pieces of intelligence information.

Given these drawbacks, scientist-critics were at a disadvantage in matching wits with the Pentagon. Nonetheless, their criticisms of the Sentinel System proved to be sufficiently barbed so that the U.S. Army decided to launch a counterattack.

The Washington *Post's* February 16, 1969, issue carried a story to the effect that the manager of the Sentinel program, Lt. Gen. Alfred D. Starbird, had proposed a "Public Relations

Program for Sentinel" to Army Secretary Stanley R. Resor. In a follow-up editorial the *Post* attacked the "Big Brain ABM Brainwash" with the description of the Sentinel public relations program:

> All of it is there—the information kits, the television films and taped radio shows, the ceaseless round of calls on Congressmen, governors, mayors, local community leaders, editors, and publishers; the articles to be written for scientific journals by Army officials and officers; the carefully prepared interviews with the press; the coordination of the whole effort with the private public relations efforts of industrial firms involved in the building of the Sentinel System.

Senator Fulbright managed to have the fifteen-page Starbird memorandum printed in the *Congressional Record*. The memorandum took note of the opposition to the Army's ABM program and defined its concept for its "Public Affairs Plan for the Sentinel Program" in these words:

> The thrust of this program will be directed primarily toward explaining the military requirements and strategic concepts inherent in the Sentinel deployment decision. As subordinate but related goals, the program will emphasize that the Sentinel System is specifically designed to meet a strategic defensive military requirement; that it is being deployed in an efficient and economical manner; that it is designed to provide a defense against a possible Communist Chinese nuclear ICBM attack through the late 1970s. . . .

Madison Avenue had moved from New York to Washington, D.C.

The Starbird memorandum proceeded to detail the various measures by which the Sentinel system would be sold to the

American people. One was of particular significance because it related directly to the scientist-criticism that had proved so harassing to the Army. In section 7c(2) we find:

> OCRD will encourage and assist in the preparation for magazine articles on the Sentinel System by civilian scientific or technical writers of national stature.

Here we have a chilling example of an agency of the Armed Forces, entrusted with weapon development, engaging in the deliberate promotion of the most expensive weapons system ever proposed. The propagandizing of the ABM system is something that should arouse the indignation of every citizen. The Pentagon already has remarkable control over the press through its orchestration of the release of information. Extension of this power to include massive indoctrination of "civilian scientific or technical writers of national stature" could be fatal to the exercise of criticism of the Military Establishment.

In the area of science, the United States has powerful instruments at hand to maintain the proper climate for independence of thought. For example, the magazine *Science* features a current commentary on the affairs of science that is lively, informative, and critical. The *New York Times* and the *Washington Post* employ full-time, highly competent science reporters. But in the area of military science, the nation is lacking in critical reporting of defense matters. No reporter has come forth to take the place of Hanson Baldwin, the military editor of the *New York Times*, who retired several years ago. Far too often, reporters based in the Pentagon become captives of the military. In many cases, the reporters assigned to cover the Defense Department are not specifically trained to take on the task of analyzing the complex issues of military science.

Many universities have schools of journalism, but they do

not turn out graduates qualified to report defense science. In general the educational institutions have paid little attention to making studies of U.S. defense problems.

When I began research on my last book, *The Weapons Culture*, which is my name for the military-industrial-political-scientific and technological complex, I thought that I might find that scholars had done much of my work for me. After all, when I started researching the book Eisenhower's warning about the "complex" was five years old.

To my astonishment I found that academics had paid no attention to the military-industrial complex. The subject jumped into the headlines in 1968 and then the universities "discovered" the complex. Harvard University was awarded a large grant by a foundation to study the military-industrial complex. Oddly enough, Harvard had for some years run a seminar on National Security Affairs; one would have thought the scholars might have looked into the rise of militarism in this country. Instead, it seemed that a good many professors were circulating in the Pentagon orbit.

This point is worth making because during the past decade the Defense Department has established beachheads on many campuses. The federal government obligated more than $1.5 billion for support of research in colleges and universities in fiscal year 1970. Even in the area of so-called basic research, the Pentagon asked for more than $300 million from Congress to spend on campus.

Two specific military beachheads on campus deserve attention.

The Defense Department has Project THEMIS which Dr. John S. Foster, Jr., described to a Senate investigating group as:

> . . . a new university research program designed to assist the development of excellence in defense-relevant research at universities not now receiving Federal or Defense support. In its first year (fiscal year 1967)

THEMIS was enthusiastically received by both you and the academic community: 173 universities and colleges submitted 483 proposals; and 50 proposals from 42 institutions representing 31 states were selected. In fiscal year 1968 we again received over 400 proposals, and have selected 43 additional centers.

Project THEMIS added twenty-five more new programs in fiscal year 1969, and funds for a like number were requested for fiscal year 1970. The actual origin of this project was a White House directive to government agencies to spread research and development funds around the fifty states on a more equitable political basis. The Pentagon got into the act because legislators were less inclined to challenge funds requested by the Defense Department.

Admiral H. G. Rickover very aptly expressed this Pentagon proclivity when he testified before a Senate committtee in 1968:

> The DOD (Department of Defense) has been able to involve itself in research having only the remotest relevance to the problems encountered by the armed services—matters at no previous time nor anywhere else in the world deemed to lie within the province of defense function—just because it has the money; it has more money than any other public agency.

The Pentagon has invaded the area of behavioral and social science research to the tune of $49.3 million of defense funds in fiscal year 1969. Under the Pentagon's dollar support, we find the University of California (Berkeley) studying "Himalayan Border Research Program" and American University (Beirut) researching "Changing Patterns in Middle East Society."

Rockefeller University received a $100,000 defense grant to study "The Psychology of Language," and Yale University got $240,000 to set up an "International Social, Political, and Economic Data Center." The Air Force underwrote a University of Chicago study of "Political Development and Modernization in Islamic Countries."

Harvard University received U.S. Air Force funds for researching a "Comparative Study of Normative Behavior, Japanese and American Youth." Incidentally, many of the contract titles are code-named so as to be indecipherable.

In the Pentagon's 1969 listing of educational contractors—an annual compilation of five hundred research and development contracts—I find that seventy-two U.S. universities each had more than $1 million in defense awards. The total amounted to $409 million.

The impact of these statistics is even greater when one reads his alma mater's annual financial report and finds that the University of Chicago lists combined operating expenditures of $211.3 million, of which $95.8 million represent U.S. government contract projects.

I remember the days before physicists discovered the U.S. Treasury, when I was a graduate student at the university. If you wanted a Geiger counter, you did not think of buying one. Rather you made it yourself. And for items that had to be procured, I recall going to Professor Arthur H. Compton. Chancellor Robert M. Hutchins thought the physicists on campus were a bunch of mechanics, with the result that funds were almost nonexistent for physics research. Professor Compton reached into his coat pocket, withdrew his personal checkbook, and wrote out a check for the electronic equipment I needed.

Today the universities are major contractors for weapons development. For example, the University of California acts as contractor for the management of two major weapons facilities—the Livermore Laboratory, a quarter-billion-dollar plant in California, and the Los Alamos Scientific Laboratory, a

100

$350 million installation in New Mexico. Annual operations for these atomic installations run close to $300 million.

No wonder that Senator Fulbright observed, "The universities might have formed an effective counterweight to the military-industrial complex by strengthening their emphasis on the traditional values of our democracy; but many of our leading universities have instead joined the monolith, adding greatly to its power and influence."

Scholars need dollars and many have become skilled operators in finding federal funds for their research. Very often this infusion of contract money into the university environment has isolated the researcher from the free interplay of the academic society. His work may be cloaked in secrecy, thus setting him apart from his colleagues and also from the students. More than once in my visits to universities, I have engaged in discussions with faculty members only to run into an academic who would withdraw from the argument by contending he knew the real facts but could not divulge them.

Some universities have become so attached to the federal government that they have established special institutions to do contract work of a specialized nature. For example, Stanford University established its Stanford Research Institute, a nonprofit organization employing almost three thousand people. Its major facility is located in Menlo Park, but it maintains offices or facilities in Southern California, New York, Huntsville (Alabama), Chicago, and Washington, D.C. Overseas offices are sited in Stockholm, Tokyo, Bangkok, and Zurich. Total contracts for Stanford Research Institute are in excess of $60 million per year.

Cornell University managed a nonprofit organization known as the Cornell Aeronautical Laboratory. This laboratory engaged in extensive research for the Defense Department, including classified work on chemical warfare agents.

This kind of research activity, although conducted off-campus, served to exacerbate student dissent. Rebellious students took matters into their own hands. On one occasion they traveled to Cornell's field facility near Springfield in western New York and stormed past security guards. They carried cameras, in violation of security restrictions, and took photographs of the installation.

Students at Cornell University and Massachusetts Institute of Technology, and at a few other institutions, focused their discontent with the campus-government ties in a "research strike" on March 4, 1969. A hastily put together organization of students and faculty took occasion to examine the misuse of science at educational institutions. I was invited to speak at several universities that day and chose the University of Pennsylvania.

I spent most of the day with students and faculty in informal discussion, informal to the point of four-letter words being commonplace. The students were deeply concerned about their role in society, about the uses for science and, most significantly, the war in Vietnam. I was struck by the fact that they were often very poorly informed about the affairs of science. They were, on the other hand, highly intelligent and motivated; I urged them to set short-term, attainable goals such as carrying on the ABM fight.

One thing that angered the students more than anything else was the presence of defense activity on campus. Their protests forced a number of universities like Columbia, Pennsylvania, Stanford, and American to dissolve campus ties with the Pentagon. For example, Cornell University "sold" its nonprofit Cornell Aeronautical Labs to the highest bidder. Stanford had to abandon its defense-supported research institute.

My impression is that the dissent on campus was very meaningful to the national debate on Safeguard. Sometimes whole science departments would sign petitions to their senators, urging a ban on the deployment of the U.S. ballistic defense system. But more often it was a lone scientist who spoke out. One such man was Dr. Wolfgang Panofsky, a fifty-year old physicist, who was born in Berlin and came to this country in 1934.

Dr. Panofsky popped up in the Senate ABM hearings as a result of a gaffe by Deputy Defense Director Packard. During the course of questioning by Senator Fulbright, the issue of independent scientific advice on ABM was raised.

The Arkansas senator stressed the fact that in the Sentinel debate the Armed Services Committee heard no witnesses other than those employed by or closely associated with the Defense Department. He prodded Secretary Packard to disclose the names of scientists with whom the Pentagon consulted on Safeguard.

Secretary Packard finally gave Senator Fulbright the name of Professor Panofsky of Stanford University. I was sitting at the press table with John W. Finney who did an excellent job of covering the ABM story for the *New York Times*. We exchanged surprised glances, knowing that the Stanford professor was an opponent of the Safeguard System. A few minutes later, Professor Panofsky came through the door of the Caucus Room and sat down to listen to the testimony. It turned out that he had an appointment with one of Senator Cooper's staff and sought him out in the Caucus Room.

Professor Panofsky's consultation on the Safeguard System was entirely accidental. On February 23, 1969, while waiting for a delayed plane departure, he had met Packard in TWA's Ambassador Club. The two men talked for about half an hour.

The Stanford physicist was then invited to appear before the Foreign Relations Committee. His down-to-earth exposition of the deficiencies of the Safeguard System impressed many senators.

Dr. Panofsky's scientific and technical credentials could hardly be challenged. His postwar activities included work for the Division of Military Applications of the Atomic Energy Commission, serving on the Air Force Scientific Advisory Board, research at the University of California Radiation Laboratory, and participation in the arms control activities of the State Department.

Other physicists, appearing before Senate committees to urge a postponement or ban on the deployment of Safeguard, included the Nobel prize-winner Hans A. Bethe of Cornell, Professor George Kistiakowsky of Harvard, and Dr. George W. J. Rathjens of MIT. Drs. Herbert York and Jerome Wiesner also spearheaded the attack on Safeguard. Dr. York served for eight years as Director of Defense Research and Engineering, the post held in 1969 by Dr. John Foster. One could hardly say that Dr. York did not bring an air of complete authority to the hearing room. As former science adviser to President Kennedy, Dr. Wiesner also displayed a competence beyond question.

The senators who listened to these anti-ABM scientists had to weigh their testimony against that presented by an opposing group of pro-ABM scientists. The views of the latter were actively promoted by a number of hard-line senators on the Joint Committee on Atomic Energy and on the Senate Armed Services Committee. Dr. Edward Teller, Hungarian-born architect of thermonuclear weapons, was an ABM champion the arms-oriented legislators could count upon. One anti-ABM senator, Marlow W. Cook of Kentucky, met with Dr. Teller for two days of discussions and was unpersuaded by his arguments. Senator Cook remarked:

> I might further state for the record that I know of no time whatsoever that Dr. Teller was ever against the expenditure of massive funds, or ever against the deployment of any major missile system that the Defense Department wanted. He is the same distinguished scientist who said, about a month or so ago, that he was delighted that man could walk on the moon, because we might well use the moon as a source for atomic and hydrogen explosions in the future.

104

Senator Henry Jackson, whose track record on promoting weapons systems parallels that of Dr. Teller, came to his defense during the Safeguard debate by raising the issue of scientists' fallibility. This line of argument might have been advantageous to the short-term goal of expediting passage of the Safeguard program, but it was a dangerous course to follow when viewed over the long term.

Scientists are not infallible. Like everyone else, they can and do make errors in judgment. But many of the great issues of today—and even more so in the future—depend on a scientific and technical underpinning. The scientific and technical future is not predictable, even by highly qualified experts. Very often the depth of the expert's specialty buries him nose-deep so that his overall vision is severely circumscribed. But expert opinion is required on technical issues, and it must be available to the legislators on an objective basis.

Senator Fulbright's subcommittee investigating Safeguard tried to bring balance into the scientists' testimony by pairing witnesses, pro and con. This technique allowed both sides of an argument to be explored before the subcommittee. Since each senator, Republican and Democrat, was permitted equal time for questioning, it allowed differences of opinion on a subject to be developed. But when the issue pertained to a future capability for a part of the Safeguard System, it must be admitted that the Pentagon always got the best of the argument. It could always invoke secrecy as a means of winning an argument on a specific matter.

Viewing the parade of pro-ABM scientists testifying before the Senate committees, I felt that most of them entered the hearing room with a real liability. Most of the Safeguard proponents were directly or indirectly associated with the Department of Defense.

For example, when one of the most articulate of the pro-ABM scientists—Dr. Donald G. Brennan—testified, Senator Fulbright queried him on his relations to the Pentagon. Dr.

105

Brennan identified himself as associated with Herman Kahn's Hudson Institute, of which he was a former president. Senator Fulbright elicited the information that the institute derived most of its income from the Pentagon.

I know Dr. Brennan to be a highly competent and sincere individual and I would not disqualify him because of his association with the Hudson Institute. He is certainly not a warmonger or a Cold Warrior; in fact, he is quite the opposite. But it would have been far more effective for the Pentagon if it had been able to produce scientists favorable to Safeguard who were not so closely tied to defense projects.

My impression is that the pro-ABM scientist who gave the best testimony before the Senate Foreign Relations Committee was Dr. Gordon J. F. MacDonald. The geophysicist, who would rate high on any scale of scientific brilliance, is vice-chancellor for research and development at the University of California (Santa Barbara). He served in 1968 as vice-president of the Institute of Defense Analyses—a wholly Pentagon-funded organization.

Dr. MacDonald's testimony on the ABM issue was effective because it was so soundly argued and fairly presented. He acknowledged deficiencies in the Safeguard System and was quick to point out specific areas in which he would like to see changes made in the program.

Almost all of the witnesses testifying on Safeguard were physicists. Ever since the development of the A-bomb, physicists have been in the driver's seat of the nation's science vehicle.

It is interesting to note how 1,216 physicists voted on the ABM issue at the time of the 1969 spring meeting of the American Physical Society. A poll showed the following results:

I *support* deployment of the present Safeguard antiballistic missile system 21%

I am *opposed* to deployment of the present Safe-
guard antiballistic missile system 76%
I have no opinion on this matter 3%
Deployment of Safeguard is likely to lead to *an increase* in the arms race 70%
Deployment of Safeguard is likely to have *little
effect* on the arms race 25%
Deployment of Safeguard is likely to lead to a
reduction in the arms race 5%
I am in *favor* of a *thicker* antiballistic missile
system 9%
I am *opposed* to *any deployment* of an antiballistic
missile system 51%
I am *undecided* about *future* antiballistic missile
systems 40%

Clearly, if this sample of the physicists was representative
of the larger community of physicists, then they were de-
cidedly against the Safeguard deployment, but somewhat more
open-minded about future systems. The senators, who listened to the physicist-witnesses, realized that the scientific community was deeply divided on the ABM issue. This left them
in the position of having to make a decision on an issue about
which scientists disagreed.

When scientists disagree in public, the public is apt to be
confused. Three Gallup polls conducted in the winter, spring,
and summer of 1969 reveal a fairly uniform pattern of public
opinion. The survey disclosed the following percentages on
President Nixon's antiballistic missile program:

In favor of the program 23%
Opposed to the program 18%
Undecided about the program 1%
Unaware of program or
have not made up their minds 58%

The Gallup poll could have been more helpful to the senators if it had shown more awareness of the Safeguard pro-

gram. I think that a complex technical issue cannot expect to penetrate deeply into the awareness of millions of Americans. They are simply not equipped by their educational background to comprehend such tough technology.

In an editorial appearing in the *Wall Street Journal* on August 6, 1969, the ABM debate was appraised. It acknowledged that "never before has the nation seen the strategic arms race debated in such breadth and detail. . . . A far clearer understanding of the strategic issues is now accessible to any citizen willing to pursue the record." Then the editors continued:

> It must be at once added that the public debate based on this vast information has been vastly disappointing. The record is there for the diligent student, but the issues were never drawn in a fashion the citizen could follow without great study. And if the ABM opponents get most of the credit for opening the record, they must also bear much of the blame for fuzzing the issues.

It seems to me that the editorial goes wide of the mark, especially if one reads further and finds that the editors feel ABM was not the real issue but that MIRV should have been.

I believe that the multiple warhead issue would be just as difficult to translate for public consumption and a far more difficult subject on which to reach a national consensus. But I feel that the ABM debate did reveal the basic issue of escalation of the arms race and this factor the intelligent citizen should be capable of perceiving and appreciating.

However, the quotation serves to raise the issue of how a technical issue can be truly subject to the democratic process. Obviously if the people, as shown by the Gallup ABM poll, are uninformed, or even uninformable, then the senators must make up their minds. Somehow or other, they must appraise the quality of the scientific and technical arguments and arrive at a decision.

For many senators such soul-searching was unnecessary; they were already deeply committed to the tradition of giving the Military Establishment whatever it asked for. The pro-Safeguard votes of arms supremacists like Senators Strom Thurmond, Barry Goldwater, and John Tower were never in doubt.

For those senators who tried to evaluate the conflicting testimony of equally distinguished scientists, the problem was one that could not be resolved by appealing to some High Court of Science. The most prestigious scientific body, the National Academy of Sciences, had closed its doors to any such appeal. The Senate, itself, had no independent mechanism for weighing the scientific and technical evidence and arriving at some conclusion.

Having listened to or read all of the Congressional debate on Safeguard, I am convinced that the anti-ABM senators argued their case well. The scientist-to-senator communication had been effective. Arguments of a highly technical character were advanced on the Senate floor. This represented quite an advance from the early days of the debate when one well-known senator was so apprehensive about technology that he was reluctant to use the phrase "ballistic trajectory" in a speech.

By the time the ABM debate peaked, many senators had absorbed much of the difficult technology and were speaking fluently about ABM, MIRV, and many other items that had been foreign to them the year before. For example, Senator Brooke, a freshman on the Senate Armed Services Committee, not only demonstrated a knowledge of the vocabulary but also of the real significance of weapons when he took issue with Defense Secretary Laird's view of the Soviet SS-9 as a first-strike weapons system. The Massachusetts legislator argued:

But in addition to a capacity for assured retaliation, we ourselves have long stressed the importance of a second-strike damage-limiting capability—it is one of the rationales the DOD applies in seeking unnecessarily accurate guidance for Poseidon and Minuteman III.

Thus, especially if the Soviet SS-9 force remains too small for an effective first strike against the Minuteman fields, what we have seen may well turn out to be an effort to acquire a damage-limiting capability, that is, a weapon system which, in the event of war, would give the Soviet Union a capability to reduce damage to itself by striking U.S. missiles.

Scientists were aided in their senatorial communications by the Council for a Livable World. This brainchild of the late Dr. Leo Szilard performed a valuable public service in making scientific advice available to senators. Szilard's council, a kind of scientist-lobby in Washington, was established in 1962 and continued on after his death in 1965. It adopted a policy of opposing an ABM deployment as early as 1964, so Szilard would have loved to see his council plunge into the thick of the ABM fray in 1968-69.

I remember lunching with Szilard at his favorite French restaurant in Washington before he set up his council. Lunch with Szilard was always something of a trial, since he would frequently change his mind about dishes and send the waiter back to the chef with an entree. He was extremely gloomy about the probability of nuclear war.

"We'll be lucky if we don't have a nuclear war in the next ten years," he told me.

His idea for a science lobby-for-peace was rather ingenious. Szilard felt that many people in the United States were worried about a nuclear war and that they would be willing to contribute a certain percent of their income to avoiding it. He thought that the scientist's "sweet voice of reason" would not be persuasive enough to senators. Therefore, he proposed

110

that a council be established to raise money and to distribute it to senators whom the council would endorse for reelection.

When I asked how much money he thought he could raise, Szilard replied without hesitation, "At least ten million dollars—maybe more."

The council never came close to such a figure, but it did succeed in raising enough money to be influential in close elections. In the case of Senator McGovern the amount was twenty-two thousand dollars one year—a very significant sum for a candidate in South Dakota.

Szilard's invention paid off in the Sentinel-Safeguard debate in the form of seminars arranged to bring scientists and senators together. For example, in the past seven years the council held forty-seven seminars, twenty-one of which focused on the ABM issue. Sixty-one senators attended these seminars and, in addition, a large number of congressional assistants and staff aides came to some sessions.

A typical council seminar might be a dinner meeting at the International Club in Washington. Usually a single scientist like Dr. Hans A. Bethe or Dr. George Rathjens would be the speaker. Rathjens was impressive because of his previous experience with defense projects such as the Advanced Research Projects Agency and the Weapons Systems Evaluation Group. Bethe's scientific stature and his long record of defense activity dating back to the wartime A-bomb project gave his words very great authority.

Pro-ABM scientists had no specific nucleation center prior to the debate over Safeguard, but they soon gravitated to the orbit of the American Security Council. This Chicago-based organization is primarily a house organ of the military-industrial complex. As far as I can determine, it is a roosting place for retired, right-wing admirals and generals who advocate massive military application of power as the answer to world problems.

In the summer of 1967 the American Security Council issued

111

its haymaker publication, "The Changing Strategic Military Balance—U.S.A. vs. U.S.S.R." Rather than appearing as a private document, it came out as a Congressional publication under the imprimatur of the House Armed Services Committee.

L. Mendel Rivers, the superhawk of the committee, wrote a brief foreword to the report, explaining that "the problem of whether the United States has sufficient nuclear weapons to meet the Soviet threats underlies our entire defense posture." An innocent reader of the report would be in no doubt that the United States lagged behind its adversary in nuclear weaponry.

Actually the American Security Council report to Mendel Rivers was a power play to push the Johnson Administration over the brink of decision on the Sentinel ABM System. It was prepared by a task force headed by General Bernard A. Schriever and included the strategic bombards, Generals Curtis E. LeMay and Thomas S. Power, along with Admirals Robert L. Dennison and Chester C. Ward. Dr. Edward Teller joined this military company.

An updated version of the council report was put forth in May, 1969, under the title "The ABM and the Changed Strategic Military Balance." This time Dr. Teller was not the solitary scientist in the military brood; ten others, including two Nobel Prize winners, allowed their names to be attached to the report.

I could not help but reflect that Eisenhower's warning about the dangers of a "military-industrial complex" included a little-noticed admonition: "In holding scientific research and discovery in respect, as we should, we must also be alert to the equal and opposite danger that public policy could itself become the captive of a scientific-technological elite."

The American Security Council is the personification of Eisenhower's "complex." Its membership includes many leaders of U.S. industry, and it makes no bones about the fact that one of its prime functions is the mobilization of U.S. business for the Cold War.

Scientists delight in expressing their findings in graphic form, and the American Security Council obliged by preparing four charts showing the comparative strategic capabilities of the United States and the Soviet Union. As a witness before Senator Gore's subcommittee investigating the Safeguard System, Dr. Teller introduced these four charts, each of which showed the United States falling behind the Soviets in missiles and bombers during the early 1970s.

Dr. Teller sadly misjudged the temper and competence of Senator Gore's subcommittee. In addition, he was not the only scientist testifying that day. Dr. Jerome Wiesner was paired with him at the witness table and was not bashful about opposing the H-bomb innovator.

The moment Dr. Teller attempted to introduce his American Security Council charts, both Senators Gore and Symington rebutted him. Senator Gore had prepared his own charts, and I know that Senator Symington had an even more detailed portfolio of graphs and tables.

The senators had done their homework, and they could no longer be snowed under by a big-name scientist. They proceeded to embattle the distinguished nuclear physicist until Dr. Teller importuned: "Sir, I would now like to ask the chairman to protect his witness from a third attack. A two-front war is all I can handle." Whereupon, he claimed the right to return to reading his prepared statement.

Gone were Dr. Teller's days of immunity from challenge. This was, perhaps, one of the most significant aspects of the ABM hearings of 1969; the Senate had gained the ability to inquire into a complex technology without being repulsed by the self-authority of expert witnesses.

The ABM battle was lost, even if by a hairline vote, but the Senate's plunge into this complex technological issue allowed it to gird itself for taking on other issues which had gone uncontested for a quarter century. It was, so to speak, the first skirmish with the entrenched forces of the military-industrial complex—with the power of the Pentagon—and it would have been incredible to have scored a quick victory against such deeply rooted strength.

Many senators distinguished themselves in the ABM debate, but I think that Senator George McGovern did an outstanding job in tackling the technology. With his wartime background as a bomber pilot, Senator McGovern could not be easily dismissed. For example, in discussing a first strike, the South Dakota senator pointed out:

> In addition, if the enemy is planning a first strike, certainly he must devise means of avoiding the great damage which he knows we could cause with some 3,000 high-performance tactical aircraft, including the F-111A, the F-4, and the Navy A-6 and A-7, which also have the ability to fly nuclear missions against a large proportion of the Soviet population, in some cases with abandonment of aircraft but not loss of pilot.

This argument was so telling that Defense Department officials simply refused to even respond to the issue.

While not a member of the Armed Services Committee, Senator McGovern demonstrated that he could effectively analyze defense matters, usually far better than most members of the powerful committee. Furthermore, the former bomber pilot introduced a new wrinkle into defense argumentation.

Drawing on the technical expertise of men knowledgeable in defense matters, he prepared an extensive list of technical questions about defense policy and hardware. This he submitted to the Defense Secretary and in due course he received a lengthy set of answers. In so doing, Senator McGovern brought into the open much information that was not forthcoming from the hearings of the Armed Services and Appropriations Committees. But more importantly he put the Pentagon on record in technical detail about controversial weapons systems and thus set the stage for a more critical examination of defense policy in the future.

In summary, it is fair to say that the Safeguard debate caused many senators to turn their attention to national security issues. It meant that they had to match wits with colleagues who had built up reputations as authorities on defense matters. When the chips were down, as the record of the Senate debates in the summer of 1969 showed, the challengers held their own with veteran members of the Armed Services Committee. It became clear that the authority of the latter was superficial and all too often they accepted the testimony of Pentagon officials without critical questioning.

The "authority" of these veteran senators derived not really from their competence in defense problems but from their political influence as reflected in their special relation to the Defense Department. That is to say, the power they possessed was on the political side of the military-industrial triangle.

VI

The Congress Shall Provide

The Constitution states that Congress shall provide for the common defense. Article I, Section VIII, specifically empowers Congress with exclusive authority "to raise and support armies, to provide and maintain a navy, to make rules for the government and regulation of land and naval forces."

There was, of course, no need for the Founding Fathers to make any provision for an air force. In colonial times no one took rockets seriously, much less the possibility of aircraft, but "the rockets' red glare" found its way into "The Star-Spangled Banner" because of British missiles used to bombard Fort McHenry near Baltimore.

Congress provided for a separate Air Force shortly after the end of World War II, and it soon became the greatest consumer of defense funds. The U.S. Air Force procures its hardware from defense industry, in this case, from the complex of aircraft, engine, missile, and electronics firms we call the aerospace industries. This complex includes such giant firms as General Dynamics, Lockheed Aircraft, and North American-Rockwell. It forms the focus of Chapter Seven where we examine some specific pieces of military hardware and their relation to national security.

Throughout the decade of the fifties the buildup of military power saw a technological thrust involving ever more ex-

117

pensive instruments of war. Individual companies became thoroughly arms-oriented and their annual sales to the Pentagon exceeded the $1 billion mark. The war industry was assuming a permanent footing in U.S. economics.

It so happened that when Malcolm Moos was working on the farewell address of President Eisenhower he used the phrase "military-industrial complex." The origin of the now-famous phrase has been given many sources by the press, but it must be credited to a small group of intellectuals who were consulted by Captain Ralph Williams, U.S.N., assigned to the White House staff. Dr. George Lowe, author of *The Age of Deterrence*, was a member of the group within which the historic set of words was coined. A Navy man himself, Dr. Lowe told me, "It's remarkable that this indictment of the military influence in America had a military origin."

President Eisenhower gave his farewell address in the form of an evening broadcast and shocked many of his old military friends by his remarks. The *New York Times* front-paged a three-column story with these words: EISENHOWER'S FAREWELL SEES THREAT TO LIBERTIES IN VAST DEFENSE MACHINE.

The story had plenty of provocation, but the press seemed reluctant to follow up on it. The next day, at his last press conference in the White House, the President was asked twenty questions. One targeted the military-industrial complex.

Lillian Levy, a reporter for *Science Service*, asked:

> Mr. President, last night you called attention to the dangers that public policy could become the captive of a scientific-technological elite. What specific steps would you recommend to prevent this?

In reply, President Eisenhower urged citizens to exercise their duties and added:

And I did point out last evening that some of this misuse of influence and power could come about unwittingly but just by the very nature of the thing, when you see almost every one of your magazines, no matter what they are advertising, has a picture of the Titan missile or the Atlas or solid fuel or other things, there is becoming a great influence, almost an insidious penetration of our own minds that the only thing this country is engaged in is weaponry and missiles.

Considering the sensational nature of the Eisenhower warning, it is strange that no one seemed to take any further cognizance of the matter. Public interest appeared to be almost nonexistent. When it came, it hit like an avalanche that had hung motionless, jammed on rocky crags, high on a mountain.

As we have noted earlier, the Eisenhower warning about the "military-industrial complex" included an additional reference to the dangers of a "scientific-technological elite."

Nowhere, however, in this admonition was there a reference to a political component of the complex. This omission was rectified in the course of a CBS television interview on November 28, 1967, in which General Eisenhower warned of the dangers of a "garrison state" and stressed the relationship between military suppliers and Congress as constituting "a tremendous influence in this country." He emphasized that "we have a whole horde of Americans who are being advantaged by being so deep in this warlike effort."

Seven years after the farewell address, President Eisenhower again spoke out on the subject of the military-industrial complex in the form of an interview with Mary Kersey Harvey, senior editor of *McCall's* magazine. Published in *Vista* (United Nations Association), the following excerpts illustrate Eisenhower's views:

Moreover, the President said, we have a situation where whole segments of the economy and the society

119

are partially or totally dependent on the billions of dollars flowing to them from Washington.

These fellows couldn't get out of it if they wanted to, the President was afraid.

Well, to begin with, there were the politicians. Every Congressman, the President explained, wants air bases, aerospace contracts, R&D establishments, military camps, and the like, for his state. And what's more, once he's got these things for his state, he'll fight to the death to see they aren't dismantled, even when they no longer serve their original or any real purpose.

Another group in the complex, the defense contractors, not only work through their Congressmen, but court the Pentagon directly.

Senator Fulbright spelled out the nature of the complex in more detail when he defined it as "the inevitable result of the creation of a huge, permanent military establishment, whose needs have given rise to a vast private defense industry tied to the Armed Forces by a natural bond of common interest."

Writing in the summer of 1968, when public interest in the complex was just beginning to stir, the chairman of the Foreign Relations Committee exonerated the military-industrial complex as having any conspiratorial component. He stated that the new American militarism was too diverse, independent, and complex for it to be the result of a centrally directed conspiracy.

Senator James B. Pearson of Kansas examined the dimensions of the military-industrial complex a year later and in a Senate speech he sketched its outline:

There are 22,000 prime contractors and over 100,000 subcontractors involved in defense business. And 76 different industries are classed as defense-oriented. Military and civilian personnel employed by the Defense

Department and defense-generated private employment account for about 10 percent of our entire labor force. Hundreds of thousands more work in retail businesses and service industries which draw vital economic nourishment from nearby defense installations. Approximately 5,500 towns and cities have at least one defense plant or company doing business with the Armed Forces. There are about 1,000 DOD, AEC, and NASA installations in this country. Three-fourths of our 435 congressional districts contain one or more major defense installations. And major segments of our economy are partially or totally dependent upon defense expenditures.

He went on to point out that managers of defense-oriented companies are strongly inclined to fight for continuation of their existing contracts and to strive for new ones. Given the nature of an elective democracy, Senator Pearson explained that it "should surprise no one that Congressmen are often under great pressure to make demands on the Defense Department in behalf of their constituents."

I describe the military-industrial-political complex as a geometrical figure, a triangle whose sides are represented by the Pentagon and by industry and whose base is the U.S. Congress. Enclosed within this triangle are the defense personnel and industrial employees in defense-based businesses. Since these people are voters and their livelihood influences the votes of their families, neighbors, and friends, one can say that a defense worker represents four or five votes. Inasmuch as it takes about twenty thousand dollars in 1970 defense funds to employ one worker for a full year, this means that a defense vote has a dollar value of four to five thousand dollars associated with it.

In a "good" year the state of California receives about $8 billion in defense-related funds. Using our dollar-vote relationship, this could involve influencing the votes of two million or more voters—a politically significant matter in a state casting 40 electoral votes in the 1968 election. When one considers that in 1968 the federal funds for defense, space, and atomic energy amounted to $28.3 billion for ten states having a total of 187 electoral votes, there is every reason why politics would enter into such contracting.

It is quite unthinkable that a wheeling-dealing politician like Lyndon B. Johnson would be unaware of the significance of such massive defense funds. During his years in the White House the state of Texas benefited to the extent that defense-atomic-space funds quadrupled to a total of $4.35 billion in 1968.

The interlinkages between defense, industry, and Congress serve to shortcircuit the democratic arrangement whereby the elected representatives are supposed to exercise a watchdog role over public expenditures. It explains why Congress was so slow in taking the Eisenhower warning about the military-industrial complex as a matter to be seriously investigated. Politicians are averse to investigating themselves. Yet they are the most formidable component of the complex, since they control the funds which the Pentagon dispenses to industry.

The war in Vietnam was the protracted event that eventually brought about a public examination of the military-industrial complex and of the role of defense in our society.

War has always been the crucial time of testing the military machine. The failure of U.S. military forces to achieve a victory in Vietnam led to public disenchantment with the Pentagon. No matter how the military or their spokesmen might try to alibi their way out of the Vietnam impasse—as, for example, claiming civilian denial of certain war objectives—the American people were dismayed that no victory was achieved or seemed within our grasp.

Until war becomes the moment of truth for a military establishment, it can claim whatever its generals and their press agents desire. The United States went into the south-eastern Asian theater as the world's mightiest aggrandizement of military power. The U.S. war machine had in the two postwar decades consumed a total of almost $1 trillion, and it boasted of every conceivable technological advancement. This tremendous aggregate of firepower and mobility and immense reserve strength was pitted against a third-rate foe.

There is no need for a recital of the events in Vietnam. Guerrilla warfare proved resistant to a weight of bomb-drops that would have flattened Germany in the last war. The fearful battle losses and the staggering costs of the war had a cumulative effect on the American people. Worsening conditions on the home front, the stressed economy, the be-leaguered ghettos, and the chaos on campus added to the public sense of discontent. But the public often finds it easier to focus on specific ills rather than on a general malaise. A series of military and technological incidents aggravated the public's concern over the war and its growing suspicion that the U.S. military machine was running out of control.

Again, one does not have to do more than list these incidents. The *Pueblo* affair off the coast of North Korea, followed by the EC-121 aircraft shootdown, raised the most serious doubts about the management of our national security affairs. The controversial TFX or F-111 aircraft failed in its military trials in Vietnam. The disclosure of the extensive use of chemical agents—$400 million worth of flame, smoke, and herbicidal agents in the Vietnam war years—shocked most Americans. Satellite-relayed television from Vietnam battle zones illuminated millions of U.S. homes with searing scenes of GIs putting the torch to native huts.

Congress was finally energized to begin making a critical examination of the Pentagon. By 1968 the costs of many technologically based projects had overrun their original estimates by a wide margin. Congressmen found that they could make headlines with investigations of military projects that involved large cost overruns. But until the fiscal year 1970 defense bill came up for approval, the Pentagon's authority was not really challenged.

More than any single event, the Senate's long debate on the Safeguard program paved the way for a concerted attack on the Pentagon's stronghold. This, in effect, was also the start of a campaign to bring the military-industrial complex under control.

Senator Fulbright led the attack on the military-industrial complex in the Senate and drew the wrath of Senator Stennis when he used the term "stooges of the military." Apologizing for overspeaking himself, the Arkansas senator said that it was no slander to mention the complex and that he, himself, merited criticism "in that, for twenty-five years, I have never before seriously engaged in an effort to cut or change, in any substantial way, the budget requests of the military establishment; nor has anyone else to speak of."

During the decade of the sixties a total of $318 billion in military contracts had been awarded to industry. This vast flow of funds emanated in the powerful Armed Services and Appropriations Committees in Congress and then ramified to industries in almost every state by the Pentagon produced fixed patterns of influence that would not be easily changed. As economist John Kenneth Galbraith put it in testimony before the Joint Economic Committee's subcommittee investigating "The Military Budget and National Economic Priorities":

> It is agreed that the Services and the weapons manufacturers decide what they want or need. They then instruct the Congress. The Congress, led by the military housecarls and sycophants among its members, hastens to comply. The citizen plays no role except to pay the bill.

124

Professor Galbraith's exposition of defense funding may seem overly harsh, but I think it is justified. After all, it was Senator Allen J. Ellender of Louisiana who said, "For almost twenty years now, many of us have more or less blindly followed our military spokesmen. Some have become captives of the military. We are on the verge of turning into a militaristic nation."

While academicians chime in today and condemn the new militarism in America, it would have been better if they had anticipated this turn of events. Actually, one American historian did just that. In Professor Alfred Vagts's introduction to his *A History of Militarism*, written in 1937, we find:

> Militarism, on the other hand, presents a vast array of customs, interests, prestige, action and thought associated with armies and wars and yet transcending true military purposes. Its influence is unlimited in scope. It may permeate all society and become dominant over all industry and arts.

The pervasiveness of militarism in America is, in part, a natural product of the free enterprise nature of U.S. industry. Americans who hold stock in war-oriented corporations are themselves accomplices in the military-industrial complex. Another large body of Americans forms a component of this complex—the nearly twenty million veterans. Although it would be grossly unfair to indict every veteran as involved in the complex, the activities of the American Legion, for example, mark it as a militaristic organization.

The key to control of the military-industrial complex lies in the defense budget. This, of course, originates in the Pentagon. The Joint Chiefs of Staff submit their combined requests for the next fiscal year to the Secretary of Defense. The latter, ritualistically, prunes back the figures, knowing that each service has asked for more than it hopes to get. The President, with the help of the Bureau of the Budget, then cuts back some more, but in the past the budget experts have been no match for the Pentagon.

The U.S. Government budget for fiscal year 1970 contains $139 billion to be appropriated by Congress. The total budget of $195 billion includes social security payments and other outlays which do not come within the framework of the annual appropriations. Defense-related funds account for about $82 billion in the fiscal year 1970 budget or approximately 60 percent of the annual appropriation. The Bureau of the Budget had about five hundred professional staff members to audit and scrutinize these vast outlays, yet only forty-five professionals were retained to study the defense budget.

We have seen that, in the case of John F. Kennedy, the military budget was dramatically increased once he became President. And Congress went along obediently with these increases.

Most recently, President Nixon expressed himself on the matter of authority in defining the military budget. In his June 4, 1969, speech at the U.S. Air Force Academy commencement exercises, President Nixon said: "The question in defense spending is 'how much is necessary?' The President of the United States is the man charged with making that judgment."

Senator Jacob Javits challenged the President on this matter of proper authority, maintaining: "In my judgment, the Senate cannot accept the exclusive authority of the President to decide on the nation's priorities and its military budget." The Senator from New York went on to raise the Constitutional issue, asserting: "I do not believe the Senate can duck this question."

In setting out to challenge the dominance of the Pentagon, the Senate and House cannot count on much help from the powerful southern appendage of the Defense Department. The Pentagon politicians have carefully nurtured the defense economies of Georgia, South Carolina, and Texas. Now that Senator Stennis heads the Armed Services Committee, one may be sure that his home state of Mississippi will become defense-affluent.

Lucius Mendel Rivers, chairman of the House Armed Services Committee, and his tough-talking chief counsel, John R. Blandford, a brigadier general, U.S.M.C.R., ride roughshod over the affairs of the committee. Chairman Rivers has seen to it that his home town of Charleston, South Carolina, boasts of every defense installation that it is possible to deploy there. Lack of space and the groundwater problem ruled out siting an ICBM base there, but a Polaris Missile Facility and the following military installations are located there: Charleston Army Depot, Air Force Base, Naval Shipyard, Naval Supply Center, Naval Station, Naval Weapons Station, Beaufort Naval Hospital, Fleet Ballistic Missile Training Facility, Marine Corps Air Station. In addition, the First District which Rivers represents contains the Parris Island Marine Corps Recruiting Depot that retains some thirteen thousand military personnel. Chairman Rivers's congressional district booms with defense affluence that illustrates the mutuality of interests of Congress and the Pentagon.

The House Armed Services Committee is supposed to analyze the annual defense posture presentation of the Pentagon and authorize appropriate force levels and approve weapons systems. The Defense Appropriations Subcommittee then reviews funds for the authorized programs and submits its recommendations to the House.

How well equipped is the professional staff of the Rivers committee to do the job of probing the military programs? This staff consists of eight men and a recent law-school graduate whose total salaries add up to $220,000 per year. All the

127

men have a military background, either of uniformed service or of civilian employment in the Defense Department. Some have additional background in the FBI or Atomic Energy Commission. Most are lawyers, but none has a truly scientific competence.

The House Appropriations Subcommittee has only five professional staff members, and they have roughly the same background as those on the Rivers committee.

I suspect that the last person Chairman Rivers would like to have on his staff would be a professionally qualified expert with Ph.D. credentials. Such an individual could prove an embarrassment to the chairman by coming up with incisive questions or factual analyses that would be difficult for the Pentagon to refute.

When I asked a staff member whether the committee had ever contracted with outsiders for defense analyses, I was told that none had ever been authorized. My reminder that the committee had printed the July, 1967, strategic analysis of the American Security Council was met with the comment, "They came to us with that report and asked us to publish it. It didn't cost us a penny."

It's all too clear that Chairman Rivers follows in the footsteps of the venerable Carl Vinson, a Georgia Democrat, who occupied the chairmanship of the Armed Services Committee for many years. Vinson's philosophy was that he was not competent to challenge the judgment of military men.

One Congressman who has contested the military wisdom is William S. Moorhead, a Pennsylvania Democrat, who shook up Mendel Rivers when he hit hard at the military-industrial complex on Walter Cronkite's television program on May 13, 1969.

Congressman Moorhead had delivered a fact-packed speech on the subject at the Sixteenth Annual Institute on Government Contracts in which he warned about "the incestuous

128

relationship between the Department of Defense and our defense contractors." The Pittsburgh representative conjured up "the symbolic but appropriate picture of a million-pound dinosaur living in a man's backyard and constantly demanding to be fed—his rationale to the homeowner is what would you do with a dead dinosaur in your backyard?"

When Chairman Rivers met Mr. Moorhead's dead dinosaur on the Cronkite telecast he was infuriated, and the next morning fired off an unprecedented letter:

May 14, 1969

Honorable William S. Moorhead
House of Representatives
Washington, D.C.

Dear Mr. Moorhead:

Last night I listened to the Walter Cronkite program on television.

Among other things, I gained the impression from your comments that you feel Members of Congress who historically have dealt with military procurement have in substance become the handmaidens of the Department of Defense and Defense contractors.

I am sure you realize that this is a very serious charge, because each of us, including yourself, took the same oath as Members of Congress.

I also consider this implied condemnation as personally directed at me as Chairman of the House Armed Services Committee, and at each Member of the Committee.

Under the circumstances, I have no alternative but to invite you to appear before the Committee to present whatever evidence you may have to substantiate your allegations.

We are in the midst of considering the military procurement authorization bill. Therefore, I hope you

129

will tell me what early date would be convenient for you to appear before that Committee.

Sincerely,

(signed) Mendel Rivers

L. Mendel Rivers
Chairman

LMR: jbs

A date was set for the showdown. This was unprecedented because Congressman Moorhead did not sit on the Rivers committee and the Armed Services Committee had never summoned nonmembers to its hearing room to air a controversy. Some people on Rivers's staff knew that it would be a mistake to act as an amplifier for the Moorhead charges. The latter's staff, spearheaded by a former Bureau of the Budget employee, Peter Stockton, scrambled to amass a weight of evidence to bolster the charges. In the process, they collected an impressive mass of evidence on how well favored Rivers's First District had become under the Pentagon's cooperation.

Mendel Rivers finally backed down. It seemed like a mini-David and a super-Goliath encounter, but in the end the Goliath of the Armed Services Committee decided that Moorhead's sling would be a potent one.

The incident serves to illustrate two points:

One, when a powerful committee is overlorded by a tyrannical chairman, a challenge may effectively be made by nonmembers of the committee.

Two, a single member of Congress still has enormous power, provided he arms himself with facts.

One might add a third point. A hard-working and idealistic staff man can research an issue thoroughly enough to aid his Congressman in prying the lid from a strongbox that many would prefer to keep locked tight. In this case, a thirty-year-old Ohio State graduate in economics did just that. Peter

130

Stockton dug hard for the facts and accumulated evidence to make a substantial case.

One of the most encouraging signs on Capitol Hill, in my opinion, is that more and more Peter Stocktons are being attracted to staff work—to low pay, long hours, and little visibility—to press for things in which they believe.

While I have selected this example from the House of Representatives, the Senate staffs are populated with equally dedicated young men and women. These people have little background in science and technology, but they are exceedingly bright and well purposed.

For example, on the staff of Kentucky's Senator Cooper, much of the anti-ABM activity was coordinated by thirty-eight-year-old William Miller. An Elizabethan scholar with a bachelor's degree from Williams and a master's from Oxford, Miller served in the State Department before joining Senator Cooper's staff. His Elizabethan background would not seem ideal for tangling with such a complex chunk of technology as that of the ABM problem, but Miller displayed an analytical approach that made for an easy mating of minds with scientists. The long ABM debate found Miller at his Senate office many nights, sometimes after midnight, but he still hopes to complete his doctorate at Harvard.

The Senate Armed Services and Defense Appropriations Committees are no more professionally endowed with talent than their counterparts in the House of Representatives. For example, the Senate Armed Services Committee has only four professionals on its staff. These men, not competent to judge the merits of highly technical issues, are assigned to the task of second-guessing the Pentagon's multibillion-dollar programs.

Moreover, the symbiosis of the generals and admirals with some of the senators saps the independence of the staff. Even if staff members were highly qualified experts, how could they challenge the organized technical might of the Pentagon, especially when their jobs depend on the favor of their chairmen? Senate staff workers point to the voluminous hearings on defense matters as constituting proof of the thoroughness of their investigations. I am the first to admit that these printed hearings are a gold mine of information, absolutely essential to the researches of any serious student of defense affairs.

I index them carefully and retain them in my library for many years as sources of valuable data on defense issues. But too often the text is marred by deletions of a security nature and by a failure of the questioners to follow up a promising line of inquiry. Too often the questions are directed to decimal-point issues while significant policy questions are avoided. But throughout the thousands of pages of testimony, it is apparent that the Senate is no match for the Pentagon when it comes to technology. Not having the technical competence to challenge military projects, the various committees tend to nitpick about rather trivial details.

In an outburst of senatorial candor, Senator Pearson asserted in midsummer of 1969:

> I submit that under present conditions it is a simple physical impossibility for the two Armed Services Committees and the two military appropriations subcommittees of the appropriations committees to effectively review and evaluate the policy and budgetary requests of the Department of Defense.

In making this statement, I am sure that the senator from Kansas would be the first to admit how diligently many Congressmen pursue their committee assignments. But the fact remains that the oversight of an $80-billion-a-year establishment—along with the many burdensome duties of elective office—does not lend itself to part-time monitoring by committees equipped with professionally inadequate staffs.

The Joint Committee on Atomic Energy, which acts as

overseer of the Atomic Energy Commission and a budget of about $2.5 billion, puts the Armed Services Committees to shame in terms of staff competence to handle technical issues.

Captain Edward J. Bauser, the committee's executive director, retired from the Navy in 1963 after twenty-two years of service. He holds an M.S. degree in physics from MIT and for eight years worked on nuclear propulsion plants. His deputy, George F. Murphy, Jr., a Harvard graduate, served eight years with the Central Intelligence Agency and then attended the Harvard Business School where he graduated in 1962. Colonel Seymour Schwiller of the U.S. Air Force, who holds a B.S. degree in mathematics and an M.S. in nuclear physics, serves with the staff along with James B. Graham, a West Point graduate with eleven years of Army experience. Graham received a Master of Science degree in bioradiology and nuclear physics from the University of California. Another MIT-trained man, Captain Francesco Costagliola, U.S.N., with over fifteen years of atomic background, aids the committee.

Atomic energy involves even more intricate technology than defense, and it should be pointed out that the Joint Committee's staff is able to talk the same language as the AEC experts. Here the committee has an advantage over other committees on Capitol Hill; it is empowered by law to be fully and currently informed on the AEC's activities.

The Joint Committee's oversight record shows that it has not been prevented from dealing with the atom's complexity because of technical incompetence. Considering the five able staff members who keep tabs on an agency with an annual budget that is about thirty times smaller than that of the Pentagon, the committees handling defense matters are immensely underpowered in technical competence.

Self-reformation is unlikely for a collective body like the U.S. Congress. Individuals and committees will be reluctant to yield even small amounts of power authority to others, be they members of a new committee or some advisory body created by Congress. Therefore, it is unrealistic to propose ideal solutions to the problem of modernizing Congress to meet the challenge of modern science and technology.

It is easy to suggest that Congress create an *independent* organization of scientists and technologists to advise it. But we already have the National Academy of Sciences, a congressional creation, and while it is independent in many respects, it is also ineffective. As in the case of the ABM issue, it ducks the really high-temperature political issues in which science and technology play a major role.

It should be emphasized that the real problem facing Congress is that of providing itself with some effective means of challenging the technological authority of the Pentagon. Obviously the Defense Department cannot be contested on an equal authority basis. For one thing, Congress would dilute the nation's pool of highly qualified professionals if it attempted to generate independent analyses of complex techno-military issues. I would suggest that the aim is not to outdo the Pentagon in such a manner, but rather to subject defense proposals and programs to careful and critical questioning as was done in the Safeguard debate.

How Congress manages to link itself to such teams of experts is obviously up to the legislators to decide. For specific issues, a committee of Congress can contract with a university for a research analysis. This depends on the willingness of the chairman to authorize the study and his ability to wrangle the necessary funds out of Congress. It is a piecemeal procedure that may be useful on some occasions, but I would not think it practical in jousting with the Pentagon.

The prolonged debate over the Safeguard program demonstrated that the Senate can absorb the basic facts about the military technology and argue the pro and con of the issue in a democratic manner. But it required an immense expenditure of energy on the part of many senators to tackle the ABM issue. And the latter is but a small part of the entire military budget. If the whole of the defense effort is to be examined more critically, it must be done more efficiently. This means that Congress must introduce some innovations into its rather old-fashioned methods of dealing with atomic-space-age issues.

The Pentagon has at its disposal powerful tools for the promotion of its defense systems. The American people and Congress have become conditioned to accept technological innovation as essential to progress—and, in the case of national security, to staying ahead of the Soviets. In this sense, research and development funds are almost sacrosanct. As we have seen, the great debate over the Safeguard program represented a manifestation of national heresy on this score.

But in more specific terms, the Pentagon has always relied on the propagation of a climate of fear in which to nurture its embryonic weapons systems. One had only to hint that the Soviets might be developing such and such a new weapon, and Congress was stampeded into appropriating funds for it.

Time after time, defense officials have used the controlled release of intelligence information, whether by leaking the data to minion reporters or by disclosing it in secret congressional sessions, to promote public and congressional enthusiasm for new weapons.

Spectacular examples of the misuse of intelligence data are to be found in the "bomber gap" and "missile gap" episodes that cost the American taxpayer many billions of dollars and may have cost us all much more in terms of arms escalation. More recently, we have witnessed the introduction of a new dimension into the gathering of intelligence data. Orbiting cameras routinely photograph large areas of enemy territory and provide "hard data" about enemy deployment of such items as ICBM sites.

Such incontestible evidence would normally be considered a stabilizing factor in the arms race, inhibiting defense officials from making exaggerated claims about enemy capability.

During the last years of the McNamara era this was undoubtedly the case.

But when Melvin Laird took over the top spot in the Pentagon, he was able to surmount the obstacle of hard intelligence by using it to anchor a base line of enemy present capability and then proceed to an extrapolation based on a maximum possible exploitation of technology. On this basis the Defense Secretary was able to project an annihilation of our Minuteman force when the Soviets acquired 420 SS-9 missiles. He simply projected a future capability based on Soviet development of multiple warheads, each having very high operational reliability and accuracy.

This shift, possibly engineered by and certainly backstopped by Dr. John S. Foster, Jr., as the Pentagon top man in research and development, marks a new departure for the military in their exploitation of the instrument of fear. I think it is what Senator John Sherman Cooper had in mind when he observed in the Safeguard debate:

> A point of view is held by some in this land which has been hardly challenged, but which we challenge today. It is that the United States is required to install nuclear systems against every threat, assumed or potential.

Unfortunately, Congress cannot avail itself of independent means to counter the "open-ended technological threat" for the simple reason that it is based on estimates of technology as it may exist in the future. No group of experts could prove in advance that a weapons system could not advance to a certain level of sophistication provided enough effort were exerted on it. Here defense officials can always respond by invoking the magic word "breakthrough," saying that some new development may revolutionize a given field of technology.

I suspect that the officials in the Pentagon are just beginning to recognize their new "instrument of fear" and that they will resort to it more frequently in coming years. The grave danger exists that it will catapult the United States into an unremitting arms race. Here Congress must not depend on technological crutches, but must rather steady itself and use common sense in dealing with the military budget. A most potent technique would be to require that the Defense Department submit a five-year programmatic budget to the Congress.

Secretary McNamara set the stage for this possibility when he introduced the concept of projecting threats and capabilities over a five-year time base. For example, his last statement before a joint session of the Senate Armed Services and Appropriations committees specified a defense program for fiscal years 1968-72. His statement had the great virtue that it compartmented funds requested for fiscal year 1968 into neat and meaningful categories. These included:

> Strategic forces
> General purpose forces
> Specialized activities
> Airlift and sealift forces
> Reserve and Guard forces
> Research and development
> Logistics
> Personnel support
> Administration
> Military Assistance Program

However, Congress needs budgetary figures projected over a five-year period for various weapons systems, both in their research and development phases, and also in deployment. Naturally, the Pentagon experts will protest that they are not magicians and cannot be expected to know five years in advance how they will be deploying forces, especially if they are still in the R&D phase.

The purpose of the budgetary exercise is to force the Defense

137

Department to give the lawmakers some indication of how weapons systems will shape up in the future so that they do not suddenly pop up in the budget as surprise items. Furthermore, this "early warning system" device will permit legislators to plan for the impact of technology without holding defense experts to a rigidly structured budget. In this way they will be prepared to debate issues of a techno-military nature before they become foregone conclusions. For example, the MIRV issue could have been forecast, had it been included in such a technological estimate of the future.

The Atomic Energy Commission, which is even more heavily committed to research and development than the Defense Department, regularly makes five-year projections of its budget. In fact, the AEC has made such forecasts for years, even in highly specialized areas of nuclear technology. This has allowed the Joint Committee on Atomic Energy to exercise a much tighter budgetary control over the AEC than the congressional committees impose on the Pentagon.

Another Pentagon objection is that such a technological forecast would tip our hand to the enemy. This could be met by proper classification of the pertinent data.

In this connection I would strongly urge that the Defense Department's custom of classifying cost data on weapons systems be brought under control. In the past the costs of even the most conventional weapons were kept secret. Now that the U.S. Senate has demanded quarterly cost accounting on the major weapons systems, there should be a scrutiny of the cost data to ascertain how much of it is justifiably classified.

In going through the voluminous congressional defense hearings, I have often been struck by the extent to which items are deleted from print due to security considerations. It is the custom for the various committees of Congress to submit their hearing transcripts to the Pentagon for security review. The transcripts are then returned with deletions in what is called a "sanitized" version.

I know of one case in which the Defense Department returned a transcript, having deleted part of a senator's questions in addition to classifying the defense official's answers. In another case, an Illinois congressman found that material he had previously cleared with the Air Force was stricken from his transcript marked "deleted for security reasons."

Very often cost data are completely eliminated from the printed record that the public gets to see. For example, page 173 of Part 3 of the House hearings on defense appropriations for fiscal year 1970 shows blank spaces for the quantity and cost of such items of procurement as: "high speed clock . . . truck . . . teletypewriter . . . dry copier . . ." However, this is very small potatoes compared to the Navy's habit of omitting cost data on a massive scale, as when they classify the unit cost of a ship.

Senator Proxmire's Joint Economic Committee has already started down the right track in demanding very specific cost data from the Pentagon. For example, in the summer of 1969 Senator Proxmire made a written request to the Defense Department for very detailed data on twenty-one weapons systems.

If the Joint Economic Committee plays its cards cleverly, it may go beyond the investigation of cost overruns on defense projects and tackle the problem of allocating federal funds to meet the national needs. In other words, barring the establishment of some other committee to deal with national priorities, the Joint Economic Committee might serve an overview function.

At the present time Congress handles the budget problem by deciding on how much the defense budget should be and then dividing up what is left among the other government agencies. But as Senator Mansfield has expressed it, there must be some balance between "external security and internal insecurity."

As a practical matter, I think that congressional control of the purse strings represents the greatest possibility for bringing the defense program under control. Tightening up the defense budget would force the Joint Chiefs of Staff to make choices in their spectrum of military projects and thus impose a self-discipline on military spending.

Control through clamping down on the military budget would require that Congress be alert to Pentagon politics that would seek to avoid cutbacks by eliminating from the budget those items dearest to the hearts of some congressmen, knowing that such economies would meet immediate protests and probably prompt restoration of funds.

One can conceive, for example, that a wily Secretary of Defense might revamp his defense budget by eliminating the C-5A Lockheed transport, knowing that this would displease the powerful Senator Richard B. Russell. Here the Secretary would have to iron out his differences with the Joint Chiefs of Staff and, in a time of a budgetary cutback, one would expect that the three services would express their individual needs in a forthright manner.

There has been remarkably little fighting between the services since the protracted conflict on the B-36, when the U.S. Air Force and Navy tangled. After that, it was tacitly agreed that each would mind its own business.

During the past decade each service has had a large enough slice of the defense pie so that it has been content to avoid coveting the others' share. But when the total pie shrinks, the portions may be too small to satisfy any of the services. It is at such a time that we may find the U.S. Navy capable of making the most searching examination of deficiencies in Air Force programs.

Vietnam war spending has, of course, boosted the defense budget to its $80-plus billion level. However, Congress must be prepared to effect control of the Pentagon's budget as the Southeast Asian expenditures go into decline. Unless this is done, the industrial component of the military-industrial

140

complex will come up with all manner of new weapons for the seventies—weapons for which we may be sure the military component will be able to devise a national requirement. There will be a strong movement to keep the defense budget at its high level. This certainly was part of the underpinning of the case for the Safeguard program.

In this connection, I find two paragraphs in President Nixon's Air Force Academy speech of June 4, 1969, most revealing. The first, which appears italicized in the *Congressional Record*, is:

> *I believe that our defense establishment will remain the servant of our national policy of bringing about peace in this world, and that those in any way connected with the military must scrupulously avoid even the appearance of becoming the master of that policy.*

The second is:

> *I believe that the basis for decisions on defense spending must be "what do we need for our security" and not "what will this mean for business and employment."* The Defense Department must never be considered a modern-day WPA.

It strikes me as though President Nixon must believe that President Eisenhower had a gift of prophecy when he warned about the dangers of a military-industrial complex more than eight years earlier.

VII

The Weapons Makers

The weapons capital of the world lies in California, concentrated in three blobs of population and industry. One is
the San Francisco Bay area, another is the sprawling megalopolis of Los Angeles, and the third is the San Diego area.
By all odds, the Los Angeles geographic complex is the citadel
of the weapons makers.

Bounded roughly by Santa Monica, San Fernando, Pomona,
and Long Beach, this California region far outranks any
other geographic spot for sheer defense statistics. In the last
fiscal year for which there are precise statistics (1968), this
area witnessed an inflow of almost exactly $4 billion in defense
funds. If atomic and space funds are included, the total federal funds pumped into this area approach $5 billion per year.

As a state, California is number one in defense and federal
affluence. The Pentagon printout of defense contracts for this
single state is impressive—128 pages listing more than five
thousand individual defense contracts for a total value of
$6.53 billion. Atomic and space funds boost the total to $8.1
billion. More than four hundred contracts are in the amount
of $1 million or more. The top ten account for $3 billion
or 46 percent of the total, reflecting the concentration of
defense contracts in the province of the very largest corporations like General Dynamics, Lockheed, and North American-
Rockwell.

If one is looking for the hard core of the military-industrial complex, it isn't difficult to find. It's in the aerospace industries that have crowded out the orange groves in California, growing fat in the beneficent artificial stimulation of the Pentagon's fiscal sun. Here we find the missile makers, the producers of aircraft, and the electronics manufacturers who depend upon the Pentagon for their business. In some companies like Lockheed and General Dynamics, the U.S. Government represents the single customer and therein lies the conundrum of the military-industrial complex.

General Dynamics, for example, is the top defense contractor with $2.24 billion in sales to the Defense Department, accounting for 85 percent of its total sales. Lockheed, with annual sales of $1.87 billion to the Pentagon, is in much the same position. These two companies account for one-tenth of the defense prime military contract awards each year. The top twelve largest defense contractors account for one-third of the dollar value of all contract awards.

Quite evidently, the making of weapons is big business—American style. This is really new to our peacetime way of life, since between wars the United States put a low priority on military preparedness. In fact, defense budgets after World War II dipped to a $13 billion annual low—a figure that prevailed until the Korean war.

Korea shot military expenditures above the $40 billion mark. At the same time, something new happened in the military scheme of things—the United States began the peacetime mobilization of its science and technology. Spurred by Korea, the technological arms race had begun. Thereafter, the Pentagon's budget exhibited increasing commitments to research and development that was dedicated to evolving new weapons of war.

When President Eisenhower took office, the defense R&D budget topped $2.5 billion and more than doubled by the time he gave his famous farewell address on the military-industrial complex. It was not only the manufacture of weapons that was big business; research and development of military hardware became a major source of income for thousands of U.S. corporations, nonprofit institutions, and universities, as well.

The extent of the U.S. dedication to weapon development is revealed by a single statistic. The Defense Department and the Atomic Energy Commission spent in excess of $100 billion on research and development in the twelve-year period ending in 1970. During the same time span, only about one-tenth this amount of money was spent on the support of basic science by the National Science Foundation and on health research by the Department of Health, Education, and Welfare. The nation's priorities were aimed squarely in the direction of national defense.

The big business aspect of defense research is illustrated by data taken from the Defense Department's latest report of the five hundred contractors performing research, development, test, and engineering work under prime military contracts. In fiscal year 1968 we find the top ten contractors were as follows:

Prime Military Contractor	Total Contract Dollars
1. Lockheed Aircraft Corp.	$918.8 million
2. General Electric Co.	573.1
3. Western Electric Co.	482.2
4. General Dynamics Corp.	429.1
5. North American-Rockwell Corp.	298.2
6. McDonnell Douglas Corp.	224.4
7. Boeing Co.	220.6
8. Martin Marietta Corp.	172.0
9. Hughes Aircraft Co.	139.7
10. Massachusetts Institute of Technology	124.1
	$3,582.2 million

If the layman thinks that private enterprise puts up its own money to develop new defense technology, he will be shocked to learn that this is a myth. For example, in the decade beginning 1957 the total amount of money spent on research and development in the aircraft and missiles industry was $40 billion. Of this private industry put up only $4.45 billion or 11 percent of the total.

In general, the nation's largest R&D contractors also head the list of those receiving the largest prime military contracts for production. Research and development is even more concentrated among the largest corporations than is production of military equipment—the top nine R&D firms account for almost half the total R&D dollars. According to the Pentagon's Directorate for Statistical Services, 85 percent of the research and development work is connected with missile, space, aircraft, and electronics programs. This substantiates the author's contention that the hard core of the military-industrial complex is the aerospace industry.

Among the nation's five hundred largest R&D contractors for the Pentagon are numbered ninety-one universities and numerous university-associated institutes. The U.S. National Academy of Sciences is listed as receiving $2.84 million in military contracts awarded by the Defense Department. Numbers of contracts and their dollar amounts are sometimes less impressive than the nature of the research being funded.

For example, Senator Gaylord Nelson of Wisconsin introduced into the *Congressional Record* (page S 9495 on August 8, 1969) a list of more than fifty universities "engaged in highly secret and dangerous chemical-biological research." He identified the research by listing ninety specific contract numbers for work at the universities and their medical schools.

The Pentagon's support of research on campus was initially concentrated in the area of the "hard" sciences, especially in physics and chemistry, but it soon expanded into many other areas, including the "soft" social sciences.

The U.S. Army, for example, entered into a contractual agreement with American University in Washington, D.C., to study the subjects of counterrevolution and counterinsurgency in Latin America. The National Academy of Sciences became involved in this work, known as Project Camelot, but subsequently washed its hands of the whole business.

The $6 million Army project ran into real difficulties as its true nature percolated through to conscience-stricken members of the academic community. In a postmortem, conducted after Camelot was cancelled, Professor Irving Horowitz of Washington University observed: "From the outset, there seems to have been a 'gentleman's agreement' not to inquire or interfere in Project Camelot, but simply to serve as some sort of camouflage." Professor Horowitz found that the Army-university relationship was not one of equals. He pointed to Project Camelot as a "tragic precedent" and concluded:

> It reflects the arrogance of a consumer of intellectual merchandise. And this relationship of inequality corrupted the lines of authority, and profoundly limited the autonomy of the social scientists involved. It became clear that the social scientist savant was not so much functioning as an applied social scientist as he was supplying information to a powerful client.

The independence of a university should be cherished by a democracy because it bears a special relationship to the vitality of a nation's free spirit and intellectual integrity. This is of cardinal importance when the flood of federal dollars poses such a potential corrupting influence on campus.

The Department of Defense finds itself in a dilemma as it eyes the great natural resource of brainpower that is concentrated in the nation's largest educational institutions. On the one hand, defense officials want to tap the highest quality talent in the land and, on the other, they recognize the danger of impairing academic freedom by exploiting this brainpower too expeditiously. The intellectual seed beds of the nation could literally be trampled into oblivion by heavy-footed policies of a weapons-hungry Pentagon.

Fortunately, this danger was recognized very early in the postwar period. Scientists feared that the university environment would become contaminated by defense funds and that the integrity of science itself would be set in challenge.

Scientists vocalized their fears loudly enough so that the federal government was forewarned of the dangers. As a result, federal agencies adopted prudent policies toward funding research on campus. The government's attitude toward the problem was also greatly influenced by the elevation of scientists to high-ranking posts in federal agencies and in advisory positions up to the White House level. Thus science buffered itself against federal maltreatment by infiltrating various echelons of government. Its main oversight was that it failed to create a persuasive representation on Capitol Hill.

I recall lunching one day with the ambassador of an Asian country and, in the course of conversation, he observed that the U.S. science representation in Congress was most undemocratic. I had to agree that there are no scientists in the U.S. Senate and—to the best of my recollection—only one *bona fide* scientist ever got elected to the House of Representatives in recent years. However, this singular individual did not manage to get reelected.

On a population basis there should be quite a contingent of scientists and engineers in Congress. Professional scientists and engineers, according to a National Science Foundation estimate, total about 2.5 million in 1970. It's probable that a great many more people consider themselves technically qualified and could be included in this community. But this group of people are not coordinated in any meaningful way to elect representatives to Congress. A number of scientists have run for Congress, but somehow or other, they do not mannage to appeal to enough voters to win office.

The United States prides itself on technological innovation—in large measure to be traced to the high creativity of science-trained individuals—and every day science and technology assume greater significance in our legislative affairs. I have often thought that if we can not elect scientists to Congress, we should have some arrangement for science representation on the committees which have a high science and technology flavor. What I would suggest is the appointment of qualified scientists for a two-year term to the Armed Services, Space, and Atomic Energy Committees.

For example, six scientists selected from the ranks of the membership of the National Academy of Sciences could serve without vote on these important committees and act as scientist-ombudsmen. Of course, an Edward Teller might get appointed to the Joint Committee on Atomic Energy, but even the National Academy of Sciences would raise a protest on such a selection. The important thing is that the voice of science would be heard in Congress. The scientist, after all, is the real weapons expert of our time and, though I would not want him to dictate national policy on weapons, I think his advice can be of critical importance.

Many people fail to realize that a scientist can rarely be fully employed by a single employer. A scientist always has a dual loyalty. He must, of course, have a responsibility to his employer, but he also has a compelling necessity to be loyal to the tradition of science. Should a scientist deviate too far from the path of truth in testifying before Congress, he runs the risk of being ostracized by the scientific community.

The fact that some weapons scientists operate within a tight circle of secrecy does not render them immune to this dual loyalty. They interact with other scientists who—so to speak— serve as proctors for the community of science that exists outside the secret area. And ultimately, when the barriers of secrecy are lifted, the insiders will be judged by the outsiders. This is the powerful corrective action that science exercises on its practitioners.

The weapons expert, like any specialist, may be carried away by enthusiasm for his work. Furthermore, the educational processes that produce today's scientists are oriented to turning out specialists, sometimes with tunnel vision and rather narrow views of society. The value judgments of a nuclear scientist may not be those we would all agree ought to be imposed on society.

Society has not yet learned how to accommodate itself to this stranger in its midst—the weapons scientist. His intellectual contribution to weaponry is essential, yet he flourishes best in an academic atmosphere where the act of exploitation may be a corrupting influence.

The wartime expedient of harnessing the brainpower of science on campus has, in some cases, been continued up to the present day with serious consequences in terms of student dissent. While U.S. industry has turned to weapons development on a large scale and many companies have become appendages to the Pentagon, the true essence of creativity still resides on campus.

It may seem a long leap from the campus to the billion-dollar activities of the military-industrial complex, but the connection is quite real. The findings in the academic research laboratory have the potential of being critically important to a weapons system or to some facet of industry that would benefit the U.S. economy.

This laboratory to application linkage is starkly evident to anyone who drives along Route 128 in an arc around Boston. Modern plants bearing unusual names like ITEK, Computer Time-Sharing, Ion Physics, Dynamics Research, Ionics, Memory Technology, Space & Tactical Systems, Signatron, and Digital Equipment dominate both sides of this superhighway. Several scores of these new plants represent the exploitation of ideas originating on campus. Many, if not most, of them are defense-supported.

Wall Street exhibits a curious schizophrenia toward these seedling R&D companies and the corporate giants like Lockheed. Though a small R&D outfit may make no profits or even have none in sight, investors snap up a public offering and evaluate the company as being worth many times its annual sales.

For example, Optical Scanning traded Over-the-Counter in 1968 for a high of $145 a share giving it an evaluation of almost $80 million; sales that year totaled $5.62 million with $1.12 earnings per share.

The skyrocketing growth of science-based companies is illustrated by the fact that American Research and Development Corporation's original $61,400 investment in Digital Equipment Corporation boomed to better than $300 million in mid-1969.

However, some of the aerospace giants illustrate the old rule that what goes up also comes down. Ling-Temco-Vought, for example, sold for a low of $11 per share in 1965, jumped to a peak of $169 in 1967, then slumped to $29 per share in 1969.

Ironically, at the moment of the aerospace industry's greatest technical triumph—the manned landing on the moon—the *New York Times* financial page bannered a story across five columns: "TO ANALYSTS OF AEROSPACE STOCKS, ALL SIGNS ARE NO GO."

Lockheed Aircraft Corporation's stock dropped to a low of $23 per share in the 1969 stock-market slide. This made Wall Street's valuation of the company a small fraction of the company's annual sales—roughly a tenth. The same was true of General Dynamics.

Why did the financial experts take such a dim view of aerospace stocks? Wall Street, needless to say, is concerned with the future prospects of a firm and it obviously assessed the potential of firms like Lockheed and General Dynamics to be very dismal. In part, this can be attributed to the general uncertainty surrounding defense business, but it must also reflect a judgment that such firms are not capable of diversifying to exploit new markets.

The gloomy view of aerospace stocks is in direct contradiction to the highly advertised claims that firms specializing in the high technology of space research will benefit from the technological fallout of the nation's space program. To my mind, these have been grossly inflated claims made by the National Aeronautics and Space Administration in order to bolster its budgetary position with Congress.

There are, of course, real benefits accruing from the U.S. space effort but they bear little relationship to the exaggerated claims of the space agency. The $25 billion spent on Project Apollo represents a massive investment in outsize engineering—in huge rocket engines, pumps, and specialized gear—that has little commercial application.

Could not these "high technology" firms convert to nondefense business and reenter the industrial economy? I would assume that the smaller firms would have this capability, but companies like General Dynamics and Lockheed have fitted themselves into an economic straitjacket. They are strapped into a special one-customer relationship that avoids the hurlyburly of the competitive market. Should General Dynamics decide to market refrigerators, it would find itself in severe competition with established companies that have production lines in operation, know the market, can distribute and service the products, and manage to make a profit.

General Dynamics would, of course, have an advantage if its defense work had produced some unique products for which the consumer market would demonstrate a real demand. With very few exceptions, however, these unique products do not exist; those that qualify are either priced out of the market or represent too small a sales volume to make it advisable to convert from defense to a civilian market.

Someday there may be a commercial market for rockets; then Lockheed could switch from making Minuteman ICBMs to—let us say—commercial rockets for carrying mail to Australia from the United States. But that day is far off and before it comes, I would think that satellite relay systems would be capable of transmitting document reproductions over intercontinental distances at reasonable rates.

There is, naturally, the civilian aircraft market, but this is highly competitive and the airlanes are starting to jam up; there is not enough commercial business for all the aerospace giants.

I think that the foregoing analysis of the aerospace industry makes understandable why some of the specialized firms like Ling-Temco-Vought are seeking to rake in more defense dollars. This is the market they understand—the one in which they feel most confident in projecting their corporate growth.

Bernard D. Nossiter, an astute reporter for the Washington *Post*, looked into the aerospace plans for the future and managed to gain access to the plans of several firms. L-T-V Aerospace Corporation, for example, opened its "Blue Book" to him. This book projects L-T-V's growth for the next five years.

As we have already noted, L-T-V shot up from position number sixty-one on the list of largest defense contractors to number seven during the 1961-69 time period. Nossiter learned that it has patterned its future on rising even higher on the list, hoping for $1.1 billion in defense work by 1973. The aerospace corporation owns only about 1 percent of the 6.7 million square feet of office-laboratory-factory space it uses for defense work; the remainder is government-owned.

In an exclusive interview with Samuel F. Downer, financial

vice-president of L-T-V Aerospace, the reporter managed to bring out into the open some of the company's philosophy on defense sales and their connection to politics. Downer expounded on this subject as follows:

> It's basic. Its selling appeal is defense of the home. This is one of the greatest appeals the politicians have in adjusting the system. If you're the President and you need a control factor in the economy, and you need to sell this factor, you can't sell Harlem and Watts but you can sell self-preservation, a new environment. We're going to increase defense budgets as long as those bastards in Russia are ahead of us.

Such corporate candor is chilling. If this is the attitude of other aerospace concerns, then is not the military-industrial complex cast in a rather sinister light? Will U.S. corporations be content to perform a purely passive role of providing requested services to the Defense Department? Or, in the course of seeking corporate growth, may they not assume a promotional attitude? We know that huge corporations maintain highly organized public relations departments, capable of disseminating propaganda on a broad scale. When aerospace firms buy full-page color ads in national magazines glorifying their products, they promote not just their companies but also the Cold War.

The real danger exists that aerospace industries, faced with cutbacks, will seek to create a climate in which the Pentagon's budget is increased. To understand that this is a serious possibility, we need to trace the economic fortunes of the aerospace industry up to the present time. In this way we may be able to sense the predicament in which the aerospace industries find themselves.

During the 1960s aerospace sales followed the pattern illustrated by the table given below:

U.S. *Aerospace Sales (1960-1969)*

	U.S. Government*	Total Sales†
1960	$13.6 billion	$17.3 billion
1961	14.4	18.9
1962	15.6	19.1
1963	16.8	20.1
1964	16.8	20.5
1965	16.9	21.7
1966	18.3	24.3
1967	19.7	26.2
1968	22.0	29.8
1969 est	23.0	28.3

* Sales to Defense Department and to National Aeronautics and Space Administration and other federal agencies. Does not include nonaerospace items.
† Includes nongovernment and nonaerospace items.

It is apparent from this summary that the aerospace industries have shown growth as a result of doing business primarily with the federal government. In the decade of the sixties, NASA accounted for $32 billion of aerospace sales and the Pentagon's total exceeded $150 billion. Up to 1965, the NASA contribution served to keep the sales curve from dipping, which it would have done because Secretary McNamara clamped restrictions on defense spending in this sector and had programmed further reductions through the second half of the decade.

In 1965 the aerospace industries were in trouble. The booster effect of Project Apollo was wearing off and Secretary McNamara's cutbacks were such that, barring other developments, government sales would be below their 1960 level.

Of course, something did happen to change this gloomy picture. The war in Vietnam provided the economic adrenalin for aerospace sales. However, as one looks back at this decade-long record of sales, the conclusion seems inescapable—except for Vietnam and Apollo, the aerospace industries did not belong in the "growth" category.

In 1970 this complex of companies is again in trouble. Apollo has been successful, but for NASA the price of success was bitter—the prospect of a reduced budget. The tapering off of the war in Vietnam threatens to dry up the flood of aircraft orders and the Congressional crackdown on the Pentagon's budget has eliminated such items as the $3.2 billion Manned Orbiting Laboratory and the Cheyenne helicopter. Moreover, the F-111 program has been pruned back by eliminating the Navy's version of this plane. All of which goes to explain why the Wall Street analysts have rated aerospace stocks in such a dismal manner.

When asked about his company's future prospects by a *Christian Science Monitor* reporter, Roger Lewis, president and board chairman of General Dynamics, replied:

> If circumstances do permit smaller military forces in the future and, therefore, a small volume of defense production, this would mean to me only an even more competitive atmosphere in which General Dynamics would work even harder to maintain a high-win rate in defense contracts.

Lewis referred to this as a "thinning out" process whereby a fewer number of companies would share the largest part of weapons development and production. However, he seeks to perpetuate the myth of competitive awards of defense contracts. The majority of defense contracts fall into the "negotiated" category and many into the "single source" cubicle.

Even when it appears that a contract is awarded on a competitive basis, one must look closely at the procedures followed. It is not unusual for a firm to be almost guaranteed a production contract if it wins a research and development award. The latter gives the R&D performer a unique advantage since it is the single parent of the evolving product. Pentagon-impregnated, the defense contractor is most likely to keep the "child" from the earliest growth stage through to maturity.

Testifying on the military-industrial complex before the Joint Economic Committee, Professor Galbraith made the following observations about the government-contractor relationship in defense business:

> I, myself, have argued that with industrial development—with advanced technology, high organization, large and rigid commitments of capital—power tends to pass to the producing organization—to the modern large corporation.

Economist Richard F. Kaufman, on the staff of the Joint Economic Committee, has studied the financial linkages between government and defense contractors. He points out that some $13 billion worth of government-owned property is used by defense contractors. This includes $2.6 billion in IPE, i.e., industrial plant equipment owned by the U.S. Government. In addition, private industry uses government-owned plants and property. Sometimes, as Senator Proxmire's investigations have brought out, this property is misused. Contractors have used this property and equipment not for the sole purpose of expediting government orders but for their own commercial work.

Defense contractors customarily receive "progress payments" from the government. These payments amount to government-supplied capital, thus liberating the contractor from the necessity of borrowing money to finance a corporate undertaking. Considering this advantage, as well as others, it becomes difficult to make a direct comparison between profits of aerospace contractors and other businesses.

All things considered, I feel that the aerospace complex represents an island of defense socialism within the national economy. This may seem like too harsh a term to apply to the aerospace contractors, but I think it is not an unfair indictment. The fact is that they bear only a faint resemblance to private enterprise in their dealings with the Department of Defense.

There are, in addition, aspects of the military-industrial complex that we have not yet considered. These include, first, the interlocking personalities that shuttle in and out of the various domains of the complex; second, the monumental cost overruns made in performance of defense contracts; and, finally, the mammoth mistakes made by both the military and industrial components of the complex.

In the spring of 1969 Senator Proxmire disclosed that one hundred of the largest defense contractors, responding to a senatorial inquiry, employed 2,072 retired military officers of the rank of colonel or Navy captain and above. The Wisconsin senator introduced into the *Congressional Record* for March 24, 1969, the following table showing the employment of high-ranking retired military officers:

Rank	Company	Number Employed Feb. 1, 1969	Defense Contracts Fiscal Year 1968
1.	Lockheed Aircraft Corp.	210	$1,870,000,000
2.	Boeing Co.	169	762,000,000
3.	McDonnell Douglas Corp.	141	1,101,000,000
4.	General Dynamics	113	2,239,000,000
5.	North American-Rockwell	104	669,000,000
6.	General Electric Co.	89	1,489,000,000
7.	Ling-Temco-Vought, Inc.	69	758,000,000
8.	Westinghouse Electric Corp.	59	251,000,000
9.	TRW, Inc.	56	127,000,000
10.	Hughes Aircraft Co.	55	286,000,000
		1,065	9,552,000,000

Speaking with reference to the military-industrial complex, Senator Proxmire warned:

> That danger is here. Whether sought or unsought, there is today unwarranted influence by the military-industrial complex which results in excessive costs, burgeoning military budgets, and scandalous performances. The danger has long since materialized. The 2,072 retired high-ranking officers employed by the top 100 military contractors is one major facet of this influence.

He called attention to the fact that almost 90 percent of all military contracts are negotiated and that a high percentage of these are negotiated with one or two contractors.

The Proxmire study revealed that the number of retired high-ranking military officers employed by defense industry had tripled in the past decade. Industry has shown a tendency to hire top level ex-military men, including officers of very high rank—up to lieutenant general level. For example, Lockheed Aircraft employs two Air Force lieutenant generals and one Army officer of the same rank. North American-Rockwell lists three vice-presidents of general rank.

Putting retired military men on a company's payroll is no crime. Many colonels or officers of equivalent and lower rank acquire considerable technical expertise in their years of military service. It would be wasteful for the nation not to tap such a skilled reservoir of talent. However, the potential for misuse of retired military men lies in their employment for purposes of influencing defense officials in contractual negotiations and in the obtaining of privileged information about weapons systems. The basic issue is one of conflict of interest and influence.

The problem is not limited to uniformed officers of the three services—as Senator Proxmire concluded in a letter

159

dated June 23, 1969, addressed to Attorney General John N. Mitchell:

> When government contracting officers and representatives—whether civilian or military—leave the government and go to work directly for a company where they have just been representing the government on contracts with that company, there certainly appears to be a prima facie case of serious conflict of interest.

The senator's letter contained specific reference to such a conflict of interest in the case of four Air Force officials and one general hired by North American-Rockwell's Autonetic Division.

The mass migration of high-ranking retired officers and officials from defense positions to jobs with private industry certainly invites the suspicion that impropriety may be involved. But this is by no means confined to a Pentagon emigration. It also involves the shuttling into and out of Washington of civilians from private industry or from institutions of higher education.

A scientist, for example, may leave an academic post to accept a position in the defense hierarchy—in the Advanced Research Projects Agency or in Defense Research and Engineering. Then, after serving for several years, he leaves the Pentagon to take a new job in private industry. Such job-hopping by scientists is not uncommon. It certainly does confer an insider's advantage on the company hiring such a defense-wise expert.

Weapons systems have grown increasingly expensive as they have become more complex and involved higher degrees of technological sophistication. Furthermore, in order to achieve a measure of technical advancement over enemy systems, U.S. defense officials have pushed the limits of existing technology, gambling that this would pay off in the future. The

R&D goal becomes one of pushing Nature's limits rather than directly competing with the Soviet technology.

Estimating the costs of such weapon development is difficult and companies anxious to win contract awards sometimes resort to the tactic of "low-balling." That is, they deliberately understate the costs, knowing that, when they overrun their estimates, they can renegotiate with a benevolent defense agency.

Congress, increasingly concerned about the high cost of weapons, lately has been subjecting cost overruns to less benevolent examination. The Lockheed C-5A Galaxy plane ran into sharp Senate criticism. Three air-frame manufacturers—Boeing, Douglas, and Lockheed—and two engine makers—General Electric and Pratt and Whitney—competed for the prize, a $2 billion contract. After the award, *Fortune* magazine commented:

> Although price and performance may have determined who got the contracts, the awards also fitted neatly into the aircraft industry's present backlog. Lockheed's Marietta plant, for instance, badly needed work and would have had to reduce operations without the C-5; Boeing and Douglas had other business.

Needless to say, it would be like thinking the unthinkable to let Lockheed's Georgia plant be idle, considering Senator Richard B. Russell's top spot on the defense totem pole.

The cost history of the C-5A reveals a tantalizing ambiguity in the way Air Force generals price out their weapons. For example, on page 347 of the House defense appropriations hearings for fiscal year 1969, Lt. Gen. Robert G. Ruegg testified that "the unit weapon system cost is $16.8 million" for the C-5A.

However, Congressmen soon discovered that the general's arithmetic did not include any R&D costs for the C-5A. On

page 373 (the same day of the hearings) we find Maj. Gen.
Duward L. Crow, director of the USAF budget, stating that
the unit price would be $25 million a copy for the first 120
aircraft. But thereafter Lockheed's costs mushroomed and
by 1970 it was estimated that the original unit price of the
C-5A had tripled.

"The almost frantic efforts on the part of the DOD," relates a panel report of the Economy in Government subcommittee of the Joint Economic Committee, "to first prevent,
then restrict, then interfere with Fitzgerald's testimony cannot obscure the facts which indicate a huge C-5A overrun, or
the fact that were it not for this courageous government employee, the overrun may have remained undisclosed."

The man referred to is A. Ernest Fitzgerald, a management
expert in the Defense Department. It takes a rugged individ-
ualist to make public criticism of Pentagon laxness in contracting; it is certainly not the boulevard to promotion. The
Joint Economic Committee uncovered evidence pointing to
a deliberate attempt at concealment of the cost overruns both
by the Air Force and Lockheed Aircraft.

As a result of publicity attending the C-5A and other military programs, Senator Stennis disclosed in mid-1969 that his
Armed Services Committee would receive periodic cost ac-
counts of forty-two major weapons systems. Also disclosed at
that time was the fact that ten major missile projects, each
representing an outlay of more than $100 million, had been
cancelled prior to deployment of the missiles. These include:

U.S. Army
    Mauler $200.0 million

U.S. Navy
    Sparrow I   195.6
    Regulus II   144.4
    Typhon   225.0

U.S. Air Force

Navaho	679.8
Snark	677.4
Rascal	448.0
Skybolt	440.0
Talos	118.1
Mobile Minuteman	108.4

It should be added that the services spent far more than these sums on military systems that were not classified as missiles or were deployed in small numbers and then taken out of inventory.

Three B-70 supersonic bombers were produced at a cost of $1.5 billion. One is on display in Dayton, Ohio, the most expensive monument of technology ever assembled. The U.S. Air Force and the Atomic Energy Commission spent well over $1 billion developing a nuclear-powered aircraft (ANP) before it was abandoned. Dynasoar, an Air Force venture into the field of space-aircraft, cost more than $400 million before it was consigned to the junk heap.

Three huge, eighty-five ton atomic cannon may be viewed at Army arsenals. They are the sole survivors of a highly publicized force of sixty monsters that cost the Army some $60 million, but involved additional very large funds spent by the Atomic Energy Commission.

Sometimes the services boldly push projects into small-scale deployment rather than admit a military mistake. For example, the United States developed two intermediate range liquid-fueled missiles, Jupiter and Thor, which it deployed in England, Italy, and Turkey early in the 1960s. Overall development, deployment, and operational costs were close to $1 billion.

Not only were these very unmilitary devices, they were in themselves risky ventures in that they invited Soviet imitation. It will be recalled that at the time of the Cuban missile crisis in the fall of 1962, Chairman Khrushchev drew the parallel between his missiles in Cuba and U.S. missiles in Turkey.

It can be argued that some of these military fiascos may be explained as the result of inadequate liaison between the scientific, technical, and military personnel involved in weapon development.

I remember attending one of the first organization meetings of the program that was to become the U.S. Air Force ANP project. At a technical session I heard engineers with almost zero knowledge of nuclear physics discuss absurd schemes for making a lightweight shield for a nuclear engine to propel a bomber.

At the time, it proved to be impossible to tell the Air Force high command that they were headed into a cul-de-sac with their nuclear bomber. This situation, fortunately, has undergone a decided change; the Air Force has sent many of its officers to graduate school, and it has also provided itself with highly qualified scientific advice at many levels in its structure.

Despite its multilayered echelons of scientific advice, the Air Force is prone to preen its prejudices for certain types of vehicles. Two of these may be singled out. One is the MOL—manned orbiting laboratory. The other is the AMSA—advanced manned strategic aircraft.

The Air Force's MOL never did manage to find a convincing military justification. In Washington circles, it is generally believed that MOL represented a sop to keep the Air Force placated because the National Aeronautics and Space Administration got the major assignment in space.

When the MOL program was approved in August, 1965, it was estimated that it would cost $1.5 billion. Like other aerospace ventures, however, it doubled in program cost. At the time of its cancellation by President Nixon in 1969, $1.5

billion had been spent or would be required to close out the
MOL space effort. It was still years away from its goal of
placing two-man crews in month-long stays in orbit.

Although many Congressmen suspected that the MOL program duplicated part of NASA's manned space flight effort,
they were unable to make their objections to this waste heard
in the space and defense committees.

The role of a military man in space was never really defined
by Air Force spokesmen but there was general agreement that
the main purpose of military men in orbit would be for
espionage—a function carried out routinely by camera-carry-
ing, unmanned satellites. The fiscal year budget (1970) contained an Air Force item of $525 million for MOL. Backing
this up on May 7, 1969, when he testified before the House
Armed Services Committee, Gen. John D. Ryan, Vice-Chief
of Staff, USAF, asserted:

> In February, the Secretary of Defense conducted a
> comprehensive review of the MOL program—its ob-
> jectives, current development status, earlier detailed
> analyses, and its relationship to NASA manned space
> projects and other DOD space activities. This review
> concluded that the continuance of the program is fully
> justified by the benefits to our defense posture antici-
> pated from MOL.

On June 10, 1969, the Defense Department abruptly announced that the MOL program had been canceled. A total
of $1.3 billion had been spent on the project that was ac-
corded such high priority by the Air Force. The House
Armed Services Committee continued its defense hearings
until August 8, but the printed record totaling 2,670 pages of
testimony has no further reference to MOL. MOL vanished
before it ever reached the launch pad, as did its apparently
great military urgency.

Other items slashed out of the fiscal year 1970 budget included:

Weapons System	Description	FY1970 Deletion	Projected Costs
SAM-D	Surface-to-air missile	$ 75,000,000	$ 2,500,000,000
———	Army heavy lift helicopter	15,000,000	1,500,000,000
E-2C	Carrier airborne early warning plane	66,000,000	600,000,000
ULMS	Undersea launch missile system	20,000,000	30,000,000,000
SABMIS	Sea antiballistic missile system	3,000,000	10,000,000,000*
RF-111	Reconnaissance aircraft	15,000,000	821,000,000
———	Light intratheater transport plane	1,000,000	1,000,000,000*
AGM-X-3	Air-to-ground missile	3,000,000	500,000,000*
Cheyenne	Helicopter air support gunship	429,000,000	1,500,000,000*
	Total	$627,000,000	$48,421,000,000

* Minimum estimates

It would be premature to conclude that all the above projects have been permanently killed. But it is clear that the future hopes of the aerospace industry were dashed by these budget slashes. Including MOL, a total of $50 billion was at stake in these defense decisions. The weapons systems represented part of the "shopping list" that the aerospace lobby planned to peddle to boost its fortunes after Vietnam.

One important project not eliminated from the fiscal year 1970 budget is AMSA, the bomber the Air Force sees as a follow-on aircraft to replace the aging B-52 strategic bombers. AMSA is certain to raise the strategic issue of the bomber versus missile role in deterrence.

When Secretary Laird made his case for Safeguard, on the basis of Phase I deployment being essential to protect hardened Minuteman ICBM silos against Soviet missile attack, he compromised the credibility of this particular deterrent system. Furthermore, the Pentagon chief advanced arguments for Safeguard that made the manned bomber look like a very weak force in the deterrent equation.

Secretary Laird argued that Minuteman silos, hardened to resist the blast pressure of three hundred pounds per square inch, were vulnerable to a five-megaton explosion. His contention was that a single SS-9 equipped with a triple warhead could knock out two Minuteman silos. Such an argument applied with devastating force to the vulnerability of B-52 bombers (or AMSAs) deployed on an airstrip. Perhaps a score of bombers would be exposed to risk, in the open, to a single SS-9 warhead. It takes only about five psi of blast overpressure to crumble a strategic bomber and put it out of commission. A five-megaton explosive delivers this bomber-crunching blast out to a distance of seven miles from its point of impact.

This high vulnerability of the bomber to a single strike was acknowledged in the course of the Safeguard debate, when Administration spokesmen specified Option 2B—protection for bomber bases against greater Soviet submarine-launched missile attack. The national system for bomber defense would add $4.2 billion to the Safeguard cost.

To my mind, there is a still more important factor that argues against reliance on a manned strategic bomber. It is the time factor of thermonuclear war. The flight time of an ICBM is roughly thirty minutes. If a first strike is made, it has to be compressed within a matter of minutes for synchronized attack if it is to succeed. Even if a strategic bomber is airborne and if the AMSA flies at three times the speed of sound, it is very much slower than an ICBM. The critical phase of a thermonuclear war could be over by the time AMSAs penetrated enemy territory.

No decision was made in 1969 to deploy AMSAs, although $100 million was appropriated for development of the new bomber. Should AMSA be authorized for production early in the seventies, the first planes would not be operational until 1978 at the earliest. At present they would be fitted with SRAMs and SCADs—missiles to overcome bomber defenses—but these weapons would probably not be very effective in the early 1980s. By that time the AMSAs, if ever employed, would be relegated to standing off enemy territory and launching much longer range missiles than SRAM or SCAD.

AMSA advocates admit that bomber defenses can be made very effective, but contend that this is an expensive counter-measure and, in fact, justifies the U.S. deployment of the AMSA system. The Pentagon's experts on Soviet bank-ruptcy have had to rethink this argument in the light of curtailed U.S. defense budgets.

AMSA advocates recognize that it is unlikely to get very close to its intended targets; they have championed the Sub-sonic Cruise Armed Decoy (SCAD) as a stand-off weapon to penetrate enemy defenses. Senator McGovern used the tech-nique of querying the Secretary of Defense with a series of incisive questions to challenge the Pentagon's justification of the new bomber.

The South Dakota legislator did more than delve into the technical aspects of AMSA, he asked questions that sought to define the role of the manned bomber in an age of missile deterrence. Although the Senate voted 56 to 32 to provide for the development of the new Air Force replacement for the B-52 strategic bomber, the right questions had been asked and the Defense Department had been forced to yield answers that allowed men like McGovern to build a new and more solid case against the Air Force AMSA.

It is possible that some Soviet strategists may interpret the U.S. deployment of supersonic bombers as meaning that the United States is planning for a first-strike policy. Some of them may actually read *A House Divided*, written by Melvin Laird when he was a member of Congress in 1962, and conclude that the U.S. Defense Secretary means what he writes. In this book, on page 81, we find: "Either a policy of first strike must be developed, together with its credible announcement, or the urgent measures of an actual underdog must be undertaken." Elsewhere, Laird defines the "first strike" in these words: "What it means is serving credible notice, and meaning it, that we reserve to ourselves the initiative to strike first when the Soviet peril point rises beyond its tolerable limit."

I do not know if the Pentagon has developed some war thermometer that has the ability to measure Laird's "peril point." Nor do I know if it would ever be loaned to the Department of State. But I do know that what Laird has written is the most dangerous kind of nonsense. Furthermore, one cannot give Laird an alibi for his first-strike mentality by saying that years have passed since he wrote his book. During the Safeguard debate in 1969 the Defense Secretary got all tangled up in talking about first strike, even maintaining that there was no doubt about Soviet intent in this respect.

Laird's alternative to the first strike—"the urgent measures of an actual underdog"—takes up a full chapter in his book. The writing seems only occasionally tangential to the rim of logic, but apparently an underdog is a kind of top dog with an inferiority complex—one who is ahead but thinks he's behind. In this chapter, Laird cautions against "nuclear parity" and recommends a policy of superiority. Nowhere in his writing does Laird acknowledge the paradox of perpetual superiority in a world in which nations seek power without limit.

AMSA enthusiasts, cornered by logical arguments about the lack of military worth for bombers in the missile era, end up by asserting that the U.S. deterrent requires diversity.

"Don't put all your warheads in one basket" is their dictum.

A "mix" of bombers and missiles has about the same worth as a diversity of money—cents and dollars. But dollars

169

are what really count in the aerospace industry's lobbying for AMSA. Faced with declining sales, and disappointed by the failure of Congress to buy many of the hardware items on the industry's "shopping list for the seventies," the powerful lobby is banking on the AMSA—and Safeguard.

Dr. John S. Foster, Jr., in mid-1969 estimated the research and development cost of AMSA as $1.8 billion. He specified a unit cost of between $25 and $30 million for AMSAs in production quantities of more than two hundred.

In a letter to Senator Proxmire, Dr. Foster wrote, "Basically, we view AMSA as an economical replacement for the B-52 bomber."

Present numbers of B-52s add up to six hundred strategic aircraft. Somehow or other, Senator Proxmire managed to find out that the Pentagon plans for more than 250 AMSAs. It is difficult to believe that these planes could be produced for less than $40 million a copy—and experience with the C-5A, Boeing's 747, and studies of the SST suggest this is a minimum figure—which would mean a total program cost of $10 billion for 250 AMSAs plus $2 billion or more for R&D. Since the mass production of the bombers would not occur until the late seventies, the real costs might approach $20 billion.

Weapons making has obviously escalated into very big business. Big, not only for specialized giants like General Dynamics and Lockheed, but also for the conventional colossi like General Electric. Although defense sales represent about 20 percent of GE's total sales, they are concentrated in divisions or corporate entities that act like separate, totally dependent-on-defense orders companies. As economist Richard F. Kaufman observed:

> . . . the tendency is for a company to enlarge its share of defense work over the years, at least in dollar value. And whether defense contracts represent 5 percent or 50

percent of a corporation's annual sales, they become a solid part of the business, an advantage to maintain or improve upon.

A company may even work harder to increase its military sales because military work is more profitable, less competitive, more susceptible to control through lobbying in Washington. The industrial giants with assets of more than $1 billion have swarmed around the Pentagon to get their share of the sweets with no less enthusiasm than their smaller brethren.

Kaufman's words scarcely make up a prescription for com placency as a democracy struggles to bring its military-industrial complex under control. The problem has become acute because of the sheer size of this complex and the inroads it has made on the American economy. U.S. defense industry now employs close to four million workers. As the *Wall Street Journal* observed:

> Most of these defense-related workers are family breadwinners. If wives, children, and other dependents are included, Americans who rely on defense work for their financial support constitute a very significant fraction of the U.S. population—perhaps nearly one-fifth.

Because of the technological underpinning of defense work, its claim on the nation's scientists and technicians is actually greater than some statistics might imply.

Dr. Arthur F. Burns, a man who is influential in the Nixon Administration, has noted that professional workers account for 16 percent of defense workers and skilled blue-collar workers constitute 21 percent of this work force. About two of every five physicists not academically employed are in defense work.

Weapons making has thus taken deep root in postwar American life. But the vast public outlays for weapons have meant constant deferral of projects designed to deal with the human problems of living in crowded cities.

By 1970 this urban neglect had become so acute that the Congress, despite its political involvement in the military-industrial complex, was forced to break out of its bondage. If we invoke the triangular pattern of this military-industrial-political complex, it seems evident that only at its political base was it vulnerable. The military and industrial interests were too great and too self-supportive to permit any attack on these two sides of the triangle.

VIII

Technology and Militarism

The rise of militarism in postwar America is associated with the exploitation of weapon technology. Research and development has become an almost unchallenged force in directing the dedication of the nation to arms. We may speak of this as technological determinism. In any event, technological innovation has revolutionized the equipment of war, changing it from the conventional military items of World War II to the hardware of the atomic, space, and computer ages.

In the case of atomic development, the war years witnessed the mobilization of scientists and engineers in the now-famous Manhattan A-bomb Project. When the war in Europe ended, the A-bomb was still hanging fire, awaiting the accumulation of sufficient nuclear material from the huge production plants to make a first test of the new weapon. The original reason for making the A-bomb was that the United States was in a race to develop the weapon before Hitler got it.

Once the war against Germany ended, the A-bomb project rolled onward without the slightest pause. There was no real thought given to halting the massive technological effort; instead, almost everyone pressed on in a crash program to make the A-bomb. As we have noted, Dr. Leo Szilard thought matters ought to be reconsidered, but he was himself tightly bound by the security rules of the A-project. Scientists had started something and they were not about to stop short of a climactic success.

If the A-bomb could be made, it would be made.

There is no need to replay Act I of the atom's violent history. The bomb was made and first tested on July 16, 1945, at Alamogordo, New Mexico. The bomb was dropped and Hiroshima was obliterated on the morning of August 6. Shortly thereafter, Nagasaki was struck and the war in the Pacific was over. There is very little evidence that President Truman suffered any agony of decision over the use of the A-bomb. A political leader had been handed a new instrument of power; it would have been surprising had the decision gone any other way.

During the early days of the post-Hiroshima period, the United States did offer to turn the atom over to an international control authority. This was the Baruch proposal, the first of a long series of attempts to arrive at some sort of atomic agreement with the Russians. Former Secretary of State Dean Acheson, one of the principals in the Acheson-Lilienthal proposals, relates:

> But the Russians turned them all down. In fact, Vishinsky said that my proposal kept him awake all night because he laughed so hard. Well, it didn't seem to me that was quite the right response to this effort. But at any rate, we did our best to have international control, and failed.

In retrospect, it seems clear that any proposals made to the Soviets, while we possessed a monopoly on the bomb, were doomed to failure, no matter how magnanimous U.S. offers might appear. The Soviets would not negotiate on such an instrument of world power as long as they did not possess the same weapon. When they did, as we learned in late August of 1949, they (and we) had a more powerful weapon in sight and the arms race increased its tempo.

The huge nuclear production plants built at Oak Ridge, Tennessee, and at Hanford, Washington, during the war turned out only a trickle of the precious A-bomb stuff before the war ended. It was just enough to fabricate a few bombs—but a few proved to be enough. Operating full blast and tuned up for maximum efficiency—which they were not in 1945—the U.S. atomic plants could turn out nuclear material for about one hundred A-bombs a year.

The early postwar years saw the atomic production so limited and sporadic that the atomic stockpile was viewed as distressingly small by some experts. There was a period of indecision and faltering as the newly created Atomic Energy Commission took over control of the militarily managed atomic project. Then it was decided that production facilities should be expanded, and three waves of plant additions and new construction were undertaken.

I remember, at the time, discussing the atomic stockpile situation with J. Robert Oppenheimer, the scientist who had successfully directed the development of the A-bomb at Los Alamos. This was before the Russians had exploded their first A-bomb. I was on the staff of George Washington University, working in the Pentagon on military aspects of atomic energy. Oppenheimer was in residence at the Berkeley campus of the University of California and was a key adviser to the military hierarchy. In those days the brilliant physicist was held in high esteem by high-ranking officers—an attitude that plummeted later when Oppenheimer was accused of being a security risk.

To arm myself for discussions with Oppenheimer, I flew out to California from Washington, carrying a case full of top secret documents. I was also armed with a revolver, carried in a shoulder holster, to "protect" the classified material. Our meeting was held in Oppie's house overlooking San Francisco Bay. Grinning at my shoulder holster, Oppie asked what I would do with it.

"Shoot myself," I replied, "if I lose these papers."

When we got down to looking at the military requirement for the future atomic stockpile, I expressed surprise at the size of it. Chain-smoking and pacing up and down the long living room of his home, Oppie muttered: "They'll never have enough of anything."

He paused in his restless tiger-walk and gazed at the Van Gogh on the opposite wall—a masterpiece featuring a unique bisection, deeply furrowed fields running counter to the sun's commanding focus in the painting.

I had no inkling then of the troubles that afflicted him— which, in fact, had their origin in the kitchen a few strides away, where some years before Oppenheimer had been approached by Haakon Chevalier, a French professor on campus. At that point Chevalier, acting for the Soviets, had asked Oppenheimer, the head of our most secret wartime laboratory, for information about the atomic project.

Haakon Chevalier approached Oppenheimer as the latter mixed martinis in his kitchen. This incident had not been revealed when I visited Oppie's house, but it was at the same spot that I witnessed an unforgettable event.

When our stockpile conversation broke up for lunch, Oppie led the way to the kitchen and took a cold bottle of Chablis from the refrigerator. Failing to pull out the stubborn cork, the great scientist sprawled on the linoleum, bracing his feet against the bottle, and grunted. My God, I thought, the man who made the Bomb is floored by a stubborn cork!

The atomic stockpile projection we discussed that day in Oppenheimer's living room was to prove almost minuscule compared to the 1970 nuclear arsenal. We had projected forward in time to the late 1950s—"the time of maximum danger" according to the Pentagon. (This time is always ratcheted forward as a periodic adjustment to threat evaluation.)

Back in the late 1940s we could not foresee that the U.S. investment in atomic facilities would exceed $10 billion by 1970. Nor could we foresee a twenty-year procurement of uranium costing in excess of $6 billion to insure the flow of raw material from which to fashion A-bombs. In fact, in the past two decades the Atomic Energy Commission has spent $11 billion for the production of nuclear material and $10.8 billion for weapons development and fabrication.

In 1970 we can estimate that the U.S. dedication to production and development of its nuclear weaponry has amounted to approximately $30 billion—allowing for some diversion of funds to peaceful uses of atomic fuel. Production of nuclear material started to climb in the early fifties as new plants came into existence and soared abruptly in the mid-fifties. Thereafter atomic production held fairly steady at a rate more than ten times higher than in the late forties.

Cutbacks in the production of atomic material—but not in weapons—began early in the decade of the sixties, dropping to a third of its peak value by the end of the decade. In 1964 the production of nuclear weapons was so great that the chairman of the Joint Committee on Atomic Energy, Senator John O. Pastore of Rhode Island, could say: "Today, we count our nuclear weapons in tens of thousands." But since Senator Pastore's announcement, the United States has spent $7 billion for more nuclear weapons.

Even in the seventies the Atomic Energy Commission is building more weapon production capacity, completing a $300 million plant addition for ABM and MIRV warhead fabrication. The AEC estimates that its costs for the Safeguard program will run to $1.2 billion. No estimates are available for AEC costs to produce MIRVs for Minuteman III and Poseidon, but they should be much more than costs projected for Safeguard.

The unremitting buildup of the atomic arsenal represents

just another example of the technological imperative—when technology beckons, men are helpless. All manner of atomic weapons were produced—from the dinosaurlike atomic cannon that were quickly consigned to the dump heap of war to the most exquisite expression of nuclear science—the packaging of many Hiroshimas in separate warheads, each assigned a predetermined target in the Soviet Union. That such technology might destabilize the arms race and undercut any hope of agreement on strategic arms limitations was beside the point. If a thing was technically possible, then it had to be done. Such was the terrible thrust of technology in the nuclear-missile era. Technology, itself, was proving to be the great enemy of arms control.

The weapons makers—the physicists in particular—who were so close to the nucleus that they could not see the electrons, had to pursue technology to its limits. Once technology became "sweet" enough to permit packaging multiple warheads in a MIRV configuration, then this had to be accomplished.

Military requirements for such a strategic weapons system would automatically, almost reflexively, fall into place. The Joint Chiefs of Staff would be informed that atomic experts had looked into the feasibility of mounting X warheads aboard a single Minuteman or Poseidon. Once this was interpreted as contributing in some way to increased firepower or to giving the United States some technological advantage over the Soviet Union, the Joint Chiefs of Staff would nod their collective heads and the military policy would be enunciated.

Geophysicist Dr. Gordon J. F. MacDonald, by no means a dove among scientists, but a man highly regarded in military circles, warned against technological determinism. Late in 1968 he pointed out:

First, technology, both in the United States and in the Soviet Union, has made available a rich array of possible

178

weapon systems, each of which possesses a much greater complexity than the primitive missiles of the late 1950s.

Second, the choices for development and deployment must be made against the possibility of disarmament negotiations. These negotiations could lead to actual limitation on the number and kind of weapons that can be emplaced or maintained and, in so doing, add new complexity to the problems facing weapons developers.

In effect, Dr. MacDonald was saying, make your weapons choices wisely, keeping in mind that you may be deploying systems that are very difficult to control.

In this connection, Adrian S. Fisher, who served as deputy director of the U.S. Arms Control and Disarmament Agency under Presidents Kennedy and Johnson, warned:

> The late George Santayana defined fanaticism as redoubling one's efforts after losing sight of one's aims. The present drive to complete the MIRV program, when the purpose for which it was started no longer exists and when the danger that it will frustrate the strategic arms limitation talks is greatly increased, seems to fit that definition

When scientists like Dr. Edward Teller become monomaniacal in their pursuit of weapon knowledge—which ultimately requires the actual testing of full-scale nuclear weapons—then this fanaticism contributes directly to militarism in our society. In this sense the weapons scientists of modern times are the ultramilitarists who propel the world into an unending arms race. When a large number of scientists are gathered together, as they are at the Livermore Laboratory near San Francisco, then a law of mass action prevails. Once these scientists turn up a new idea or concept for a new weapon, their enthusiasm carries them on to persuading authorities to approve projects to prove out their brainstorming.

It has been said that scientists are like little children in that they never lose their sense of wonderment and inquiry. Science is the pursuit of new knowledge—a pushing back of the barriers that separate today from tomorrow.

Looking at a particular weapon design, an expert sees a possibility for a new approach—one that might yield a lighter or a more efficient nuclear explosive. This scientist does not think of himself as a weapons maker, certainly not as a militarist. He is merely doing his job the best way he knows how. I have found that most of these experts are almost clinical in their detachment from any sense of horror associated with the kill-power or ultimate use of their brainchildren.

It is someone else's job, these professionals maintain, to look into arms controls. But just whose job it is has never really been very clear. Today, largely as a result of the initiative a few scientists took in this regard, we have an Arms Control and Disarmament Agency which, in theory at least, is supposed to look into these all-important matters of arms controls.

But because President Kennedy was so cautious and President Johnson didn't give a Texas hoot about arms controls, the fledgling arms control agency has never really gotten off the ground. Its pitifully small budget—an emblem of bureaucratic authority—has been continually sniped at by hawkish Congressmen who seem terrified at the prospect of peace. Thus when a truly critical issue of arms control came into focus—the funding of a massive ABM program and the entering into a new domain of weaponry—the Arms Control Agency remained ossified. It was a stillborn dove with unflexed wings.

We should not expect the Defense Department to be much interested in disarmament; that is not its business. As Richard Goodwin expressed it in his *New Yorker* essay:

> It represents a constituency against arms control, not because generals want war or oppose disarmament on principle but because their necessary professional cau-

tion demands that they overestimate every advantage of a potential opponent and underestimate their own capacities. In narrowly professional terms, it is inevitable to estimate that any agreement is risky, even if the only reason for doing so is an assumption that the other parties to it would not agree unless agreeing gave them an edge.

Political leaders piously mouth many expressions of their firm belief in disarmament, but they always entwine the olive branch with thorny qualifications. For example, in mid-1969 President Nixon said:

> *I believe we must take risks for peace—but calculated risks, not foolish risks.* We shall not trade our defenses for a disarming smile or honeyed words. We are prepared for new initiatives in the control of arms, in the context of other specific moves to reduce tensions around the world.

But in this very same speech, President Nixon obliquely attacked some of his critics on the score of "unilateral disarmament." And he also pointed to the fundamental issue of deciding "how much is necessary" in defense spending. Nuclear sufficiency and arms control bear an Ike-Mike relationship.

The Joint Chiefs of Staff will argue against putting any faith in an arms control agreement unless they feel that the security of the United States is not jeopardized by these arms arrangements. But since the military chiefs are professionally oriented to thinking in terms of "worst possible" and "maximum feasible" or "greater than expected" threats, they are hardly likely to feel secure under any conceivable conditions of arms control. This situation is now aggravated in the extreme by the uncertainties posed by weapons technology and its undefined future performance.

181

The two giant nuclear powers seek some kind of *modus vivendi*—some sort of stability in which neither can strike first at the other without certainty of an annihilation-response. In other words, each side requires an assurance that nuclear deterrence will prevail. The situation was described in colorful terms by J. Robert Oppenheimer in 1953:

> We may anticipate a state of affairs in which two Great Powers will each be in a position to put an end to the civilization and life of the other, though not without risking its own. We may be likened to two scorpions in a bottle, each capable of killing the other, but only at the risk of his own life.

The line-of-sight confrontation of two scorpions, each aware of the other's raised stinger and its lethality, is an oversimplification of today's situation. The weapons systems that constitute the intercontinental "stingers" are highly complex, and each side is necessarily uncertain about the other's capability. Furthermore, each power must think years ahead in laying its own strategic plans which, in turn, affect the other's. The technological enhancement of missile kill-power has thoroughly muddled the whole arms control issue.

The planet Earth is starting to wobble under its overburden of armaments. Man's "wonderful inventions" have placed at the disposal of five nations destructive power so great as to benumb the mortal mind. A third nuclear scorpion, Red China, has gained entry into Oppenheimer's bottle. It threatens to perturb the twofold equation of deterrence, for a threesome of nuclear powers is a nervous company.

The Soviet Union, sharing thousands of miles of disputed borders with Red China, must wonder how its oriental neighbor perceives the threat of nuclear retaliation. Other Asian powers, particularly India, cannot help but ask whether they can depend on U.S. nuclear deterrent power if they face a showdown with China. India lies in the threat-shadow of missiles that could arc across Nepal over distances easily covered by intermediate range ballistic missiles. India must, therefore, ponder the decision to "go nuclear" and build up its own stockpile of nuclear weapons and delivery systems. Such a decision would make heavy inroads on the Indian economy. The current defense budget of India is about $1.5 billion; huge additions to it would be required for developing ICBMs capable of striking at China's heartland.

While the United States, the Soviet Union, and Communist China constitute the three major nuclear powers, other non-nuclear countries like India and Japan are involved in the interplay of deterrent forces. Red China's limited nuclear power, even before it acquired a long-range missile capability, was perceived as a strategic threat to the United States and was used as a justification for the Sentinel ABM System. It still remains as an "optional threat" for Phase II of the Safeguard System. Once the Red Chinese nuclear stockpile is deliverable by missiles, it will undoubtedly become a much more significant factor in the military calculations of both Russia and the United States.

In the meantime the two nuclear giants confront one another and, sensing more complex and less controllable situations in the future, they argue over arms controls. Throughout the first quarter century of the nuclear age, the two great powers have not been able to come to any agreement on limiting their strategic arms. Admittedly, they have been able to reach some limited agreements bearing on arms development, but these have not cut deeply into the grain of the military problem. No side has yet denied itself any potential weapons or limited their numbers on a quota basis.

The first major agreement among the world powers was the Limited Nuclear Test Ban Treaty of 1963. I remember hooking on to Adlai Stevenson's campaign train in the summer of 1956 when he first drew serious national attention to the test ban issue. It was my first exposure to national politics. Even though a political amateur, I sensed that Stevenson's campaign issue was not a vote-winner. I knew that the candidate, making his second run against Eisenhower, understood this, too. But he persisted in airing the issue because he believed it to be of paramount importance to the control of the international arms race.

When the two great powers got around to discussing the test ban, the stumbling block to negotiations was the inspection problem. The United States was unwilling to enter into a test ban agreement unless it had at its disposal the means of verifying tests the Soviet Union might make in violation of the treaty. Technological considerations made it relatively easy to reach agreement on systems to inspect for nuclear tests in the ocean, in the atmosphere, and in the near reaches of space. But underground tests were a different matter. Small nuclear detonations, especially if conducted in certain areas where earthquakes are common, might not be identifiable as such.

"No treaty, however much it may be to the advantage of all," said President Kennedy, "however tightly it may be worded, can provide absolute security against the risks of deception and evasion."

These risks could have been minimized if suspicious events were subject to "on site" inspection—that is, by having teams of experts visit the suspect areas and look for evidence of an illicit underground test.

The Russians were adamant on this score—they equated such inspection with outright espionage. In the end, underground tests were allowed as long as they did not throw amounts of radioactive debris into the air to contaminate neighboring territory.

The Limited Nuclear Test Ban Treaty did not arrest the march of weapons technology. For example, the United States and the Soviet Union have conducted hundreds of underground tests since the treaty went into effect in 1963. Some of these are in the megaton range. But the treaty has served, barring minor contributions from France and China, to limit the radioactive burden of the atmosphere. The United States will be testing its Spartan warhead, for example, until at least 1973 and defense experts have assured Congress that underground tests will allow adequate development of the new weapon.

The United States and the Soviet Union were also able to come to terms on another nuclear agreement—the Treaty on the Non-Proliferation of Nuclear Weapons. The prime purpose of this treaty is the prevention of the spread of nuclear weapons around the world. This is obviously in the interests of the major nuclear powers and presumably also of non-nuclear nations. But the treaty does not strike at the heart of the problem—the limitation of strategic weapons systems. However, Article VI of the treaty reads:

> Each of the parties to the Treaty undertakes to pursue negotiations in good faith on effective measures relating to cessation of the nuclear arms race at an early date and to nuclear disarmament, and on a treaty on general and complete disarmament under strict and effective international control.

Over the years both sides have self-righteously gone on record as being in favor of disarmament, the United States often in rather specific terms and the Soviet Union usually in a more general manner. Everyone rather sanctimoniously speaks of the need for general and complete disarmament, but few steps are taken on this GCD road. In fact, the test ban treaty and the nonproliferation agreement are rather modest steps—ones not seriously contested by the Defense Department. However, the question of limiting strategic arms is a big step and the Pentagon can be expected to vigorously resist such arms restrictions.

At that time it appeared the two nuclear giants would get together for arms talks. President Johnson and Chairman Kosygin both released statements on July 1, 1968, indicating that the road was open to such talks. These SALT (strategic arms limitations) talks were set for scheduling just as the Soviets invaded Czechoslovakia. (Au. note: Late in 1969 Russia and the United States finally met to hold arms talks.)

By the time the Czech dust settled, certain events in weapons technology had marred the chances for reaching agreement on a MIRV test ban. The U.S. Air Force had made a sufficient number of MIRV tests to make it very doubtful that the Soviets would feel that a test ban might impose any restrictions on this weapons system. They could argue that the U.S. experts had learned enough to go ahead with deployment of Minuteman III and Poseidon, as, indeed, official Defense Department statements on MIRV production contracts would indicate.

Pentagon experts, on the other hand, could claim that while the Russians had conducted fewer MIRV tests, continued testing might escape U.S. detection. Furthermore, MIRVing the SS-9 missile system conferred a far greater advantage on the Soviet strategic strike forces than we could exploit with our lighter weight missiles.

If a MIRV test ban could not be executed, then it followed that each nation would have to assume the other would proceed to multiply its missile warheads to the maximum extent. This multiplication process poses the greatest of complications for negotiating a strategic arms limitation.

The reason lies in the impossibility of finding out by means of national systems how many warheads an in-silo missile mounts. U.S. orbital inspection procedures have been developed to a high degree of precision. They can ferret out missile silos anywhere in the Soviet Union. The U.S. Air Force launches a satellite "inspector" every few weeks and keeps accurate tabs on Soviet missile deployment. Skilled photointelligence (PI) specialists can compare sequential photographs and deduce a great deal about Soviet missile capability. But PI men cannot see what a silo cover conceals. Even if, by some unlikely chance, both countries could agree on periodic "open hole" inspection by orbital cameras, the technical problem is too difficult for orbital espionage to penetrate a nose cone and determine how many warheads are inside.

A senator once asked J. Robert Oppenheimer how he would go about detecting hidden A-bombs.

"If you hired me to walk through the cellars of Washington to see whether there were atomic bombs," replied Oppenheimer, "I think my most important tool would be a screwdriver to open the crates and look."

Not even the most optimistic arms control expert believes that the Soviets will let an American get close enough to an ICBM to use a screwdriver.

This means that the MIRV inspection problem is essentially an impossible one. This, in turn, means that hopes for arriving at some limitation on deployed ICBMs are very dim. The essential reason for this pessimism is to be found in a statement of the problem by Dr. Harold Brown, now president of the California Institute of Technology. Writing in the spring issue of *Foreign Affairs* in 1969, the former secretary of the air force and SALT negotiator put it this way:

> An agreement to limit strategic forces would have to continue to preserve mutual deterrence. It would have to provide for force structures that would make it impractical for either side to approach a first-strike capability, either by altering forces covered by the agreement or by increasing forces not so covered.

Suppose, to illustrate the nature of the technological nettles swarming around the MIRV issue, we assume that the Soviets would by some miracle agree to freezing strategic missiles

187

at their present levels, when as an approximation we could say that the total number of missiles is roughly the same on each side. This puts the U.S. total at 1,710 and the Soviet force at 1,600. These inventories apply to January 1, 1970.

Could the U.S. accept such a weapons freeze? Could the Russians?

From the U.S. viewpoint, it has to interpret the first-strike capability of the Soviet missile force as defined by Dr. Harold Brown. The fly in the strategic ointment here is that the Soviet missile force is a mix of about three hundred SS-9s, eleven hundred SS-11s and 13s, and over two hundred SLBMs.

U.S. strategists would argue that in time the three hundred SS-9s could mount a total of three thousand warheads and be capable of knocking out 95 percent of the Minuteman force. And they could argue further that the Soviets might hit upon some technique for taking out our SLBMs. They would, accordingly, make the most vigorous objections to any such missile freeze.

From the Soviet viewpoint, their experts could impute a very high accuracy to the Poseidon system so that it poses a first-strike capability against Soviet missile sites. They could say that nearly five thousand Poseidon warheads could be thrown at Soviet targets plus a minimum of three thousand Minuteman III warheads—possibly six thousand if the ICBMs are uprated. Thus hardheaded Soviet analysts could protest any such missile limitation.

Might it not be possible to cut back missile deployments to a level that would satisfy both sides so that neither had a first-strike capability? Sliding back the missile deployments automatically reduces the number of aim points for a first strike and thus this stratagem does not solve the problem. Even if it did, the problem of inspecting the operational missile sites as to the quality of the siloed missile would remain. A mere orbital census of missile sites is not enough; one has to have an actual warhead count—and this, as we have seen, is a dream in the views of most arms controllers.

This being the case, it would appear that the only hope for reaching some agreement on strategic arms limitations lies in the area of defensive weapons.

The prospects for limiting ABM deployments are not bright because there appears to be no *quid pro quo* for negotiation. The Soviets have deployed less than a hundred Galosh interceptors around Moscow to protect part of its population. The United States is in the process of deploying several hundred Spartans and Sprints around Minuteman fields to protect ICBMs. This is an asymmetric situation, both in defense worth of the systems and in time. We could, I suppose, agree not to deploy any ABMs if the Soviets would agree to decommission their Galosh system. But this hardly seems an attractive enough deal for the Soviets to accept.

Technology thus emerges as the true barrier to arms controls. Both sides have bowed before the dictates of an imperious technology and have failed to appreciate that they were deploying systems quite hostile to control.

Given protracted negotiations at the SALT conference tables and a lack of any specific agreements, is the arms situation utterly hopeless? Will the arms race run completely out of control so that in the mid-seventies we may face an even greater expansion of weapons?

Judging from the history of modern weapons, they obey their own imperative, spiraling upward into new domains of ever greater cost and complexity. But it is this combination that has led Congress to have second thoughts about armaments. Furthermore, many legislators have done their homework—studying the new weapons until they are no longer in the dark about them—and they cannot be intimidated by industry salesmen and military promoters. The mood of Congress has changed, as evidenced by the Senate's prolonged debate over the Safeguard System and by its continuing skeptical appraisal of other weapons systems.

There is also a growing awareness that twenty-five years after Hiroshima the atomic stockpile is of awesome proportions and that further expansion of it is unlikely to alter our national security.

Fundamentally, however, the nation's legislators must respond to the need for changing the national priorities. This means shifting funds to domestic needs, rather than funneling them to the Pentagon. When this is done, the military-industrial complex will experience the only real control that a democracy can impose, namely, cutbacks in funds supplied to the Defense Department.

Therefore, I believe that it is possible for self-control—for prudent and rational adjustments of our own armaments—to have a profound influence on the arms race. As we advance into the later years of this decade, the force-field of Red China's nuclear power will alter the bipolarity that has produced such lock-step arming on both sides of the Iron Curtain. The Soviet Union must inevitably configure its military priorities to confront the immediate threat defined by forty-two hundred miles of a troubled border.

It is entirely possible that the two nuclear giants will not enter into any formal agreements to limit their strategic arms. But I think that as each nation takes a more reasoned view of its nuclear might and of the consequences of unleashing it, each may moderate its pace of arming. Here the United States must understand that continuation of an arms-beyond-doubt policy serves to instill doubt in the minds of others. We need to replace this with a policy of rational armament.

I realize that such a proposal can be met with the angry charge of "unilateral disarmament"—a cry that has in the past been sufficient to whip up opposition to any reductions in the Pentagon's budget. The counselors of fear have long prevailed. Edmund Burke once wrote: "No passion so effectually robs the mind of all its powers of acting and reasoning as fear." The many fingers of fear have clutched the nation for two decades and have converted us into an armed society.

We must pry away the clutch of fear that has enveloped us—that has sponsored the precipitous rise of a new techno-militarism in America. In so doing we can return to the great works of construction of which America is capable and for which its moon-touching talent is so well adapted.

The control of a dictatorial weapons technology has become the nation's most urgent problem. Already it encompasses our lives. Its hidden fruit lies deeply buried in a thousand prairie sites. It would ring our decaying cities with a chain of killer-missiles to fend off an attack that would usher in "mankind's final war." It would seduce to its temple the keenest minds of our society. America would in the process become a fortress with ramparts stretched from shore to shore, bracketing a garrison state.

In a democracy the ultimate weapon against a technological imprisonment of the nation is the bright flame of criticism. We stand in no danger of a military coup that would rob us of our liberties. The new militarism has a soft glove over its iron fist. Yet it threatens the land, feeding on fear and exploiting fear until, as President Eisenhower observed in his farewell address: "The total influence—economic, political, even spiritual—is felt in every city, every state house, every office of the federal government."

The grave danger of such dedication to and envelopment by arms is that they will control us. Such a war industry generated in Japan in the thirties; the weapons makers became the architects of Pearl Harbor. The real safeguard today, the true deterrent, is the root knowledge that nuclear war has no victor.

I had more faith in the form of deterrence—as it were, an automatic death certificate—when the apparatus of nuclear destruction was less computerized and more subject to human control. The lumbering strategic bomber of the 1960s had the great merit that it could be commanded to fly a mission until it reached a fail-safe point of no return. Several hours were available to ascertain the nature of an attack and even to deal with the machinations of a Dr. Strangelove.

Deterrence in the 1970s depends on ballistic missiles whose swift course through the blackness of space leaves only minutes of decision time. The defensive situation in command and control of Spartan interceptor missiles is so critical that we are progressing to the point where the decision to launch missiles becomes the impersonal province of the computer. Missile technology has pounced on man with a vengeance, even robbing him of his decision-making role.

Technology is running out of control, sweeping all before it and diminishing man every day. The raped atom makes our largest cities candidates for instant oblivion. The ballistic missile compresses time and makes of war an unplayable game. The computer intrudes into the mind-space of man so that his cortical creation becomes his competitor. And the great scientists, whose sparks of intellect made a lump of matter a blaze of energy, are in awe and fear of what they have done. They see civilization trying desperately to plot its coordinates of the future. Yet nowhere are there charts or pilots to reckon the course.

Meanwhile, despite the challenge and uncertainty, society limps along in its slow pace, beset with a multitude of old problems and numbed by the impact of a rampant technology. The old ways of man and the new technology are in strange and fierce contrast.

The situation facing the world is no different from that described by Albert Einstein, when he was visited by a reporter in September after Hiroshima. Still vacationing at his Saranac Lake hideout deep in the woods, Einstein had pondered the meaning of the Bomb and concluded:

As long as there are sovereign states with their separate armaments and armament secrets, new world wars cannot be avoided. In my opinion, there is no other salvation for civilization and even for the human race than the creation of a world government with security on the basis of law.

Almost a quarter century has passed. Nuclear war has not blighted the earth, but man's practical progress toward the theoretical goal of world order has been antlike.

Today the flame of fear persists. And men and nations arm for war; its very instruments have become part of our economy. Science, the quickening force of the century, has found its greatest expression in works of war. We arm as no nation in history has ever armed itself. Other nations seek the same arms.

We arm not just beyond doubt, but beyond belief. We arm for a weapon war in which all men are victims. No poets can sing of arms, as Virgil once did. Our science has petrified the poets.

Glossary

ABM—Antiballistic missile.

A-bomb—A nuclear weapon deriving its energy entirely from fission of heavy elements.

ABRES—Acronym for the work on advanced ballistic re-entry systems done by the Advanced Research Projects Agency. These are designed to allow U.S. warheads to penetrate enemy defenses.

ACDA—Arms Control and Disarmament Agency.

AEC—Atomic Energy Commission.

Aerospace—Adjective that applies to the complex of industries, including aircraft, space, missile, and electronics.

Ajax—Also Nike-Ajax. An early U.S. missile designed to protect U.S. cities against bomber threats.

AMSA—Advanced manned strategic aircraft. Bomber under development to replace the B-52.

ANP—Aircraft, nuclear propulsion—acronym for U.S. Air Force project to develop a nuclear-powered bomber.

Antimissile—Class of missiles designed to intercept attacking missiles.

ARPA—Advanced Research Projects Agency. A high-level Department of Defense research agency.

Atlas—Liquid-fueled, early Air Force intercontinental ballistic missile, now obsolete for military purposes.

B-52—Heavy, long-range bomber of the U.S. Strategic Air Command.

B-70—Experimental supersonic Air Force bomber. Three

195

planes were produced prior to cancellation of the project.

BMEWS—Ballistic missile early warning system. This consists of three huge radar installations designed to give twenty-minute warning of a missile attack.

Breakthrough—The name given to a technological development that is revolutionary in its impact.

C-5A—Air Force code for the Lockheed Galaxy supertransport.

Camelot—Project name for Department of Defense social studies program with American University.

CEP—Circular error probability. A measure of missile accuracy. Defined in terms of the radius of a circle within which 50 percent of the missiles impact.

Counterforce—Refers to operations or capability aimed at destroying an enemy's strategic strike forces.

Discrimination—Process whereby a defender separates true warheads from decoys.

DOD—Department of Defense.

Dynasoar—Air Force space-aircraft designed for controlled reentry through the atmosphere. Now canceled.

Empty holes—Applies to possibility that a first strike may find the missiles attacking empty silos, i.e., corresponds to a launch on warning.

Exoatmosphere—Space beyond the earth's atmosphere. Corresponds to zone for Spartan missile interception.

F-111—A series of aircraft developed for Air Force and Navy use. The Navy version has been canceled.

First strike—An attack of a preemptive character designed to eliminate an adversary's strategic strike forces.

Galosh—Soviet antiballistic missile deployed around Moscow.

Hardening—Process for protecting a missile silo or military installation against all but a very close warhead impact.

Hercules—Also Nike-Hercules. A U.S. Army short-range missile developed after Nike-Ajax.

Hiroshima bomb—An A-bomb with an explosive equivalent of fourteen kilotons.

ICBM—Intercontinental ballistic missile.

JCS—Joint Chiefs of Staff.

Jupiter—A U.S. liquid-fueled intermediate range missile once deployed in Italy and Turkey.

Kiloton—Explosive equivalent of one thousand tons of TNT.

Livermore Laboratory—Weapons development laboratory of the AEC, administered by the University of California.

Los Alamos Scientific Laboratory—An AEC facility near Santa Fe, New Mexico, where the first A-bomb was developed.

Manhattan Project—Code name given the U.S. A-bomb project during World War II.

Megaton—Explosive equivalent of one million tons of TNT.

Minuteman—Solid-fueled ICBM deployed in underground silos in states west of the Mississippi. An early, single-warheaded version (Minuteman I) is being replaced by MM II. This in turn is being followed by Minuteman III with MIRV warheads.

MIRV—Multiple, independently targeted reentry vehicles. Minuteman III incorporates three MIRVs and Poseidon carries as many as fourteen.

MOL—Manned orbiting laboratory. An Air Force satellite program canceled in 1969 after incurring costs of $1.5 billion.

MRV—Multiple reentry vehicles. A cluster of warheads incorporated aboard a single ICBM. The RV is not individually aimed.

MSR—Missile site radar. Designed to guide Sprint and Spartan missiles to their intercept point.

Nagasaki bomb—An A-bomb dropped on the Japanese city of Nagasaki in World War II. Its yield was twenty-one kilotons.

Neutrons—Penetrating nuclear particles released in nuclear processes such as fission or fusion.

Nike-X—Code name given to a system designed to provide a thick defense shield against a heavy attack on the United States. System is still under development by the U.S. Army.

NORAD—North American Air Defense Command.

OTH—Over the horizon radar. A type of radar that detects distant missiles by means of back-scatter effects.

PAR—Perimeter acquisition radar. A Safeguard radar designed to acquire the track of incoming ballistic missiles fifteen hundred or more miles from their targets.

Parity—A condition said to exist when each party in an arms race acquires nearly equal strategic strength.

Pen-aids—Penetration aids. Devices or techniques aimed at allowing warheads to penetrate enemy defenses.

Plasma—A sheath of ionized particles. Also called the fourth state of matter.

Polaris—Name given to the U.S. Navy's submarine-launched ballistic missile force.

Poseidon—A MIRVed version of Polaris, carried on converted Polaris-type submarines.

PSAC—President's science advisory committee.

R&D—Research and development.

RU—A reentry vehicle containing a nuclear warhead.

Safeguard—Name given to the U.S. ABM system approved by Congress in 1969.

SALT—Strategic arms limitations talks.

SCAD—Subsonic Cruise Armed Decoy. A stand-off weapon designed as a penetration aid for the AMSA bomber. SCAD acts as a decoy by appearing on enemy radar as a bomber. It is armed in the sense that it carries a nuclear warhead.

Second strike—Generally used to describe a retaliatory strike launched after an enemy strikes first.

Sentinel—U.S. ABM System announced by the Defense Department in 1967. Modified in 1969 and renamed Safeguard.

SLBM—Submarine launched ballistic missile. Examples: Polaris and Poseidon.

Soft site—An unprotected missile base or a city.

Spartan—The U.S. area-defense ABM. Designed to intercept attacking warheads at an altitude of over one hundred miles. An essential component of the Safeguard system.

Sprint—The short-range missile interceptor designed to explode its low-yield nuclear warhead in the earth's atmosphere down to an altitude of ten thousand feet above sea level.

Sputnik—A Soviet satellite. Sputnik I orbited the earth in October, 1957.

SRAM—A short-range attack missile that forms part of the weapons system of the G-H type B-52 bomber, the B-58 supersonic bomber, and the FB-111 bomber, and is designed to penetrate heavy terminal bomber defenses.

SS-9—A heavyweight Soviet strategic missile. Rated by U.S. authorities as capable of throwing a single twenty-five-megaton warhead or three five-megaton MIRVs.

SS-11—A liquid-fueled Soviet strategic missile with a warhead of one megaton.

SS-13—A solid-fueled Soviet strategic missile with a warhead less powerful than the SS-11.

THEMIS—A Defense Department program for sponsoring basic research at U.S. universities.

Thor—An intermediate range ballistic missile once deployed in England.

Titan—A heavyweight U.S. strategic ICBM. Titan I has been phased out, but Titan II is still deployed as part of the U.S. strategic force.

Warhead—Name given to the nuclear explosive of a missile.

X-ray kill—The mechanism involved in exoatmospheric interception of an attacking warhead.

ZAR—Zeus acquisition radar.

Zeus—Also Nike-Zeus. A U.S. Army missile designed for ballistic missile defense. Spartan represents an improved, longer-range Zeus.

APPENDIX I

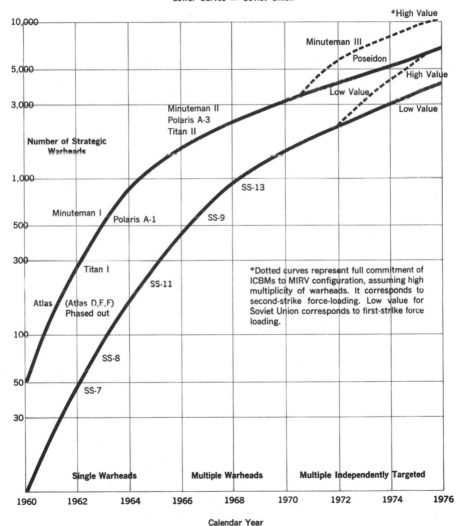

Ballistic Warhead Force Loadings (1960-1976)
(ICBM + SLBM + MIRV + MRV)
Upper Curves = United States
Lower Curves = Soviet Union

Calendar Year

201

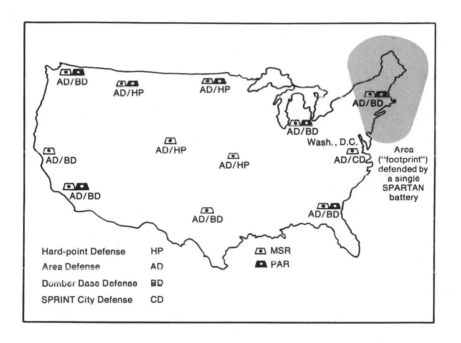

AD/BD

AD/HP

AD/HP

AD/BD

AD/BD

Wash., D.C.

AD/HP

AD/HP

AD/CD

Area ("footprint") defended by a single SPARTAN battery

AD/BD

AD/BD

AD/BD

Hard-point Defense	HP	⬛ MSR
Area Defense	AD	⬛ PAR
Bomber Base Defense	BD	
SPRINT City Defense	CD	

INDEX

205

INDEX